MW00596789

CAMPING

AN EXPERIENTIAL GUIDE

GENA,

THANKS FOR YOUR SUPPORT AND INSPIRATION!

Allan C. Clark

Allan C. Clark

Camping: An Experiential Guide

ISBN (Print): 978-1-54396-712-8
ISBN (eBook): 978-1-54396-713-5

DEDICATION

I have been blessed to have had an amazing camping partner for a number of years. Carmen, my friend and former wife, has accompanied me to the deepest, darkest parts of the forest as well as to a number of very fancy campgrounds. It was Carmen's idea to name some of our camps, usually for their most memorable attributes. One was "Rainy Camp" for fairly obvious reasons, while another was "Baby Camp" because of the seemingly huge number of screaming infants who were there. Other camp names include "Eagle Camp," "Fishhook Camp," and "Bear Camp." Each camp had its unforgettable moments, but sometimes just getting to them was an adventure, itself. Driving on a precarious dirt road bordered by a two-hundred-foot drop was at times hair raising. Motoring down a highway with a pull-behind camping trailer that shuddered violently whenever a semi passed was also unnerving. Journeying on back roads at nighttime during a torrential rain was a formidable experience. Nonetheless, throughout our camping adventures and despite Carmen's having to tote heavy loads, despite her becoming impaled by a fishhook, and despite her enduring the threat of an impending tornado, Carmen has been the best camping companion anyone could wish to have. Through our adventures together, Carmen has contributed greatly to much of the content of what is presented here and so it is to Carmen that I dedicate this book.

PREFACE

The boy struggled to remain upright as the horse clopped slowly up the mountain trail. He held fast to the belt that was looped onto his father's jeans. The boy's dad was in love with fly fishing and particularly enjoyed fishing in waters where native trout could be found. This often meant driving to someplace near the headwaters of various mountain streams and sometimes even required the renting of pack horses to get to the best spots. This was one of those trips. This was in the upper reaches of Sequoia National Park and I was that boy.

I grew up knowing only two kinds of camping: pack horse camping and car camping. From each gleaned numerous memories that remain with me still. Some of my earliest memories are of me as a toddler watching Dad as he left camp with his fly rod and empty creel leaving Mom and me waiting impatiently for his return. When he came back to camp Dad's creel nearly always held the freshest, most delicious trout anyone could ever want. I remember camp breakfasts, not as much for the cornmeal battered trout as for the "coffee." The "coffee" I was given consisted mainly of milk to which a spoonful of sugar and a splash of camp coffee was added. True, it wasn't the real thing, but for me to have "coffee" at that young age was enormously special, making me feel like a "big boy."

Car camping was often a rather spontaneous event when I was a kid. Dad and Mom would sometimes decide upon a camping trip the night before, figuring upon a quick stop along the way at a grocery store. Equipment consisted of little more than a tent, sleeping bags, a lantern, a two-burner stove, and some fishing gear. In the summertime Mom usually kept on hand a spare pound of coffee, an extra pound of butter, a small bag of a flour/cornmeal mixture, and couple of extra cans of pork and beans. Milk, bacon, bread, eggs, sardines, and a box of Bisquick were among the few other necessities to be purchased along the way if they weren't already in her larder. As you may imagine, pack horse camping required a bit more advance planning.

For a few years both of my parents were very active "den parents" for a Cub Scout group of which my older brother was a member. Being a couple of years younger – too young for official membership – I was dubbed a "sub-Cub" and as such I attended all of the meetings and participated in most of the activities. I also carefully studied all of the Cub Scout manuals, virtually memorizing much of the camping information they contained. I also enjoyed reading all of the camping tips I gleaned from my brother's subscription to "Boy's Life Magazine." Many years later I was happy to stumble upon a book called, "The Golden Book of Camping and Camp Crafts" by Gordon Lynn and illustrated by Ernest Kurt Barth, containing a collection of many of those same timeless camping tips. I treasure it along with a myriad of other books on camping, survival skills, edible and medicinal plants of the wild, and so on that I have read and/or collected over the years. I also have an extensive collection of guides to all kinds of animals, trees, and wildflowers. Favorite authors include Tom Brown, Thomas Elias & Peter Dykeman, and Bradford Angier.

Over the years I have explored a wide variety of camping options including backpacking, canoe camping, car camping, and in recent years, RV (Recreational Vehicle) camping. Although my camping experiences have been limited so far to adventures within the continental United States, I feel sure that much of what I have learned could be applied to camping elsewhere. I have slept under the stars or in an old fashioned "umbrella" tent, in a survival-style shelter, under a tarp lean-to, and in a number of other kinds of shelters and tents as well as in a few RVs. I will confess that some attempts were more successful than others; but will also submit that I tried to learn from whatever mistakes I made. You will find only fleeting references here to camping in the snow, despite the happy tales friends have told about their snow-camping experiences, Snow camping only interests me in terms of survival situations that I pray will never happen to me.

I will attempt here to give some thoughts applicable to various kinds of camping while at the same time pointing out some errors I have made or have seen other campers make. My hope is that by writing this guide I can help you to avoid such mistakes and to aid you in becoming a better camper.

DISCLAIMER

Prudence dictates that except where specifically noted, all of the information given here is offered as guidance only. What is written here is not meant as a formal treatise on the subject. Nothing in this document should be construed as being completely factual nor without possible error. The book has been written entirely as a general guide using my own experiences and knowledge along with what I have absorbed through reading or have learned from other campers I have observed. It is my hope that anyone reading this book will understand its intent and will make use of the content offered as a simple overview of methods, procedures, information, and cautions I have learned and observed through decades of camping.

A LITTLE HELP FROM MY FRIENDS

Probably most people imagine that a book is entirely and solely the work of the author. Without going through the process, themselves, they cannot conceive of the many steps involved in a book's production. Help for this work has come in many forms. Many thanks are due to countless anonymous strangers who unwittingly demonstrated the wrong way to camp. Some very good campers have shared their experiences and knowledge freely and generously with no notion that portions of their wisdom might someday appear in book form. I'm especially grateful to have had a fine camping companion with whose help I have learned so much about a variety of camping styles along with many of the blessings and pitfalls of each.

On the more technical end of producing this volume, I must say a few words about my publisher. Giving birth to this book has some parallels to childbirth. From conception to holding the final product in my hands has been filled with anxiety and anticipation. The hours of hard work that have gone into bringing this book into the world have at last been rewarded. I am convinced that my publisher made the birthing process far easier than it could have been.

I imagine few people ever pay much attention to the "thanks to" part of most books. I will admit to having been one of those who usually skipped lightly past all of that in order to get to what I thought was the important part of the book. I'm beginning to understand now why authors feel it important to acknowledge those who helped to bring an author's book into being.

My thanks to those few who took the time to read the manuscript and who suggested changes in both punctuation and content. I wanted to name names, but was asked to refrain. I also greatly appreciate the many contributions made by my friends in "My Campfire Group" on Facebook, where I posted portions of the manuscript for discussion and feedback.

Most of all, I am grateful to my parents. Mom showed me by example how to make delicious meals using little more than an iron skillet, a campfire, and basic ingredients. Dad demonstrated numerous aspects of camp craft and outdoor skills. Both parents taught me so much about camping and about appreciating the many wonders of the outdoors. I am sure their spirits can be found within the pages of this book.

THE BIG QUESTION: WHAT DO YOU THINK OF AS CAMPING?

Perhaps the most important question is: What is camping to you? Do you bring everything with you including the kitchen sink or do you "rough it?" (Someone once told me that their idea of "roughing it" was a night in a hotel without room service.) While there are the basic divisions of RV camping and tent camping, even those have sub-categories or some additions that might not leap to mind when contemplating those differences. RVs can range tremendously in size and style. There are luxury, Class A "pushers" that are at least as big as or even bigger than city buses and can contain a washer and dryer and even an artificial fireplace. There are also tiny "teardrop" pull-behinds so small that you have to wonder where anyone can possibly sleep in one. Somewhat in contrast, I've seen tent campers who paid the extra fee for a site with an electrical outlet so they could plug in the microwave oven they brought along. I have seen more than one tent camper who had installed a converter for a 120-volt outlet in his car toward the goal of rigging up his DVD projector in order to view movies on a 5′ by 8′ portable screen.

By contrast, I have seen others who brought little with them other than a tiny tent, a sleeping bag and pad, and a small pot in which to boil water for tea or to cook a small, freeze-dried item for dinner. There are some people who seem to think that camping must somehow include having a television upon which to watch "the game." For others it is an opportunity to escape the trappings of city life, to appreciate the comparative silence of the outdoors, and simply to be in a peaceful place where they aren't confined by walls. I have enough of a foot in both camps to address most of the spectrum between the two, but I lean heavily toward the latter. Although I am writing this book mainly for tent campers who camp with family members or friends, I will also include information I believe important to those who prefer to do their camping in recreational vehicles.

After numerous attempts to "pound it to fit" it finally sank into my brain that no two camping trips were ever the same, sometimes requiring very different equipment and nearly always calling for a different mindset. Each camping trip is its own adventure, filled with countless opportunities to overcome whatever adversities your undertaking may present. It has been said that anyone who claims to have been so well prepared that nothing whatsoever went wrong, is probably lying. It is my belief that one of the things that makes camping interesting and sometimes challenging is dealing with the adversities. Did you forget to bring the can opener? Now what will you do? It is pouring down rain when you arrive at your campsite. How will you deal with that? Some of the most pleasantly memorable camping adventures I have ever experienced were filled with problems like these.

One very dark and horribly rainy night after a harrowing four-hour drive, Carmen and I arrived at our somewhat remote destination only to discover that it was raining so hard we couldn't even find the campsite. Despite the relentless downpour we somehow managed to locate a place in which to park our pickup. There was little choice but to spend the night in the truck. Being careful not to run down the pickup's battery too much, we found a very satisfactory radio station and a quick dash to the rear of the truck supplied us with the means for pleasant imbibing. With the fine bunch of music playing in the background we chatted and chortled (and sipped) until we finally fell asleep. To this day we still look upon that as one of our favorite camping memories.

It is my hope that by reading this book you will feel comfortable enough with your knowledge and abilities to create many new camping adventures. And if circumstances bring about some adversities you will know how to be flexible enough to find ways to transform misfortunes into times you, too, will fondly remember.

WHY GO CAMPING?

I believe the fun of recreational camping is most likely found in its departure from the norms of daily life and in the successful overcoming challenges. In your daily life you don't usually pitch a tent or gather kindling or perform any number of the tasks involved with camping. It's different. Camping as a process is filled with unfamiliar moments and even a few challenges at times. You may find it difficult to find a flat enough area to use as a campsite. What will you do? You discover that two tent stakes have vanished. What now? Your youngest child just waded through a patch of poison ivy. How will you deal with that? Most of your eggs got broken in transit. What will you do about that? Anything might suddenly challenge your ingenuity, but at day's end you will sit back and mentally pat yourself on the back because you worked through it and figured it out.

Some kinds of camping are a bit easier than others but they all entail a great deal of planning, a lot of packing, the purchasing of supplies, and varying degrees of effort in setting up camp once you arrive. Nonetheless, there is a feeling of self-reliance that comes with camping that you just don't get elsewhere. Camping, especially tent camping, is work - sometimes hard and hot work.

While canoe camping on a blistering hot afternoon Carmen and I at last arrived at what was to be our riverside camp. Hours on the river in the relentlessly hot sun had sapped our energy. We were well roasted and extremely weary. Setting up camp was something neither of us felt energetic enough to do. We decided to cool off a bit first. I went for a quick dip in the river and Carmen waded a bit near the shore. Since there were no trees close at hand, we decided to erect a sheltering tarp as a place in which to shade ourselves for long enough to regain our strength. Finally, we felt ready to put up the tent, to gather some firewood, to unpack enough food for dinner, to get the campfire going, and to cook our evening meal. Believe it or not, it was fun!

When you return home at the end of your normal, daily routine, your house or apartment is there, ready for your arrival. When you camp you may have to "build" and furnish your home when you arrive. Where you normally reside if you are hungry you can choose to pop a ready-made meal into the microwave or even phone an order for food delivery. At a restaurant there are people who cook your meal for you and others who will even pour your wine or coffee for you. But when you camp whatever needs to be done, you do it - no matter how difficult. When your trip is over you can feel that you truly accomplished something and that all, or most of what you did, got done through your own efforts or through the efforts of you and your crew. You got through it, probably enjoyed it greatly, and may even have figured out that you and/or your bunch are much better at camping than you may have imagined!

WHERE SHOULD YOU CAMP?

A number of factors can influence the answer to this question. If you are leaving right after work then you need to calculate what is available within the radius to which you can drive in order to arrive well before sundown. For instance, if you can't get home before, say, 5:30 p.m. and you still need an hour to pack the car, that means you can't be on the road until 6:30 p.m. If sundown is at 8:30 p.m., for example, that means you should plan to camp somewhere within an hour's drive. In that way you will have plenty of time before dark to set up the tent, to gather some kindling, to get a fire going, and to break out the marshmallows. Of course, this would only be possible if you had the foresight to pack some sandwiches to have for dinner *en route* or were willing to make a quick stop at a drive-thru on your way out of town. Consider the time limitations as you plan your trip. Maybe you are just fine with pitching your tent or parking your RV in the dark. Remember, though, to check to see if the campground has a gate that is closed at a certain hour. You would certainly kick yourself (possibly with a lot of help) if you were to arrive only to discover that the campground's gate had been locked. Of course, if you were to be able to leave home at some time in the morning your radius of possible camping destinations would expand greatly.

Consider also what sort of camping you want to do. Some campgrounds, especially private campgrounds, cater almost exclusively to recreational vehicles and seem to only offer tent sites as an afterthought. One campground I experienced only offered tent sites in an area far distant from most of the RVs and in the muddiest, most mosquito-infested part of the campground.

What interests you?

Think about what you expect to do when you camp. Do your interests and those of your companions run toward hiking, fishing or swimming? Which campgrounds feature those things? Are you interested in geology, history or music? Does the area near the campground hold anything of this kind that you and your bunch might enjoy? A little advance research into such possibilities can pay big dividends - especially if inclement weather gets in the way of other activities.

Are you roughing it?

If "rough camping" or backpacking suits your style you are very likely to find what you need in a not-too-distant national forest or even state forest. In most instances you will discover that camping is free or quite nearly so, requiring only that you register with a ranger prior to your stay and that you practice "leave no trace" camping.

How about paddling to your camp?

Canoe camping can be a wonderful adventure for couples or even for a small group. Check with local outfitters for available options. Of course, if you're really wanting to get away from it all you will likely need to contact more distant outfitters or even professional guides. River trips outlined by outfitters can take as little as a few hours, with camping offered adjacent to the outfitter's store, or as long as four or five days, or even longer depending upon how much navigable river there is. Many outfitters, besides offering canoes and shuttle service, can even supply all basic camping equipment except food for a package price. Bear in mind this usually includes little more than a tent, sleeping bag(s), lantern, and possibly a camp stove. Some outfitters also carry a limited stock of typical foods that may be useful, such as, marshmallows or canned stew, usually at convenience store prices or higher. A little meal planning and advance purchasing is probably best.

If you plan to camp beside the canoeing waters you should be sure the landowners are okay with doing so. Outfitters can often supply information about potential campsites. Some can even supply maps showing specific sites authorized by landowners. Approved campsites may be limited, making it advisable to arrive early to stake your claim. It must be noted that the number of landowners who allow camping is rapidly diminishing because of careless campers who leave behind trash or other mess that the landowners must clean up.

Know before you go.

It is important to get a clear understanding of the outfitter's shuttling procedures. Good outfitters keep careful track of their clients and exhibit great concern if the trip takes much longer than what they consider normal. If you plan an overnight camp during what the outfitter designates as a 12-hour float, you should make it known. Otherwise the outfitter is likely to suspect a mishap of some sort. Some not-so-good outfitters are known to become belligerently impatient. I have had one call out from the shore, demanding that I curtail my fishing so that he could get his shuttle vehicle back to its home base. With that in mind, I have found that the very best canoe or canoe camping trips were those whose end points were actually at the outfitter's location.

WHEN SHOULD YOU CAMP?

I suppose the facetious response to this question would be: Whenever you can! However, you may be limited by a wide variety of factors. What time of year works best for you? In other words, would you and/or your family enjoy camping in the colder months? What are the opening and closing dates of the campground you might choose? When can you take vacation days from work or can a weekend camping trip consisting of a couple of overnights be sufficient?

Far from the madding crowd...

If you want a bit less of a crowd around you at a campground then if possible, avoid weekends, especially holiday weekends. Consider planning your arrival for a Monday or at least sometime early in the week. Except when holidays fall during the week, you are most likely to find your chosen campground to be sparsely or even very thinly populated Mondays through Thursdays. If at all possible, call the campground office directly somewhat in advance of your departure. You may discover that on the dates you have in mind the entire area around your campsite is slated to be filled with nearly a hundred pre-teen members of the Pink is Perfect Society and that might not suit your plans.

Do you think it might rain?

Weather can also be a deciding factor. Before finalizing your plans, be sure to check the long-range weather forecast to get a good idea of what weather to expect during your proposed camping trip. Check the forecast again on the day before your trip. Keep in mind that most campgrounds have policies requiring a minimum of a 24-hour notice of cancellation in order for you to receive a full refund on your reservation.

CHOOSING A CAMPGROUND

Much depends upon your expectations. How do you plan to spend your time at that campground? Do you envision simply sitting under a shade tree with a good book or do you plan to do some wildlife photography? If you are bringing family or friends then what are their interests? Are there activities that your kids might enjoy? Is there a pool, beach, or fishing pier? Are there any presenters of wildlife information, nature interpreters and/or guided hikes? Or would the whole family enjoy a hike to a waterfall?

It is best to phone ahead to get a clear understanding of the layout and clientele of a potential candidate for your camping adventure. It would also be a good idea to discover what amenities the campground might have such as hot & cold water showers, a game room, or even a source for ice cream. Knowing whether the campground has firewood available might be important.

Recently I learned of a campground at which the adjacent fishing/swimming/boating lake's dam sprung a leak. The lower water level affected all of the water-related activities. This is a good example of why it is important to call ahead to your prospective destination to check local conditions that could affect your camping adventure.

Campground Fliers and Maps

When you check out a campground online or when you actually arrive at a campground it is nearly certain that you will encounter a list of rules. Most often online they will be found in a PDF file, or at the campground, on a printed flier or on some other handout. Read them. Those fliers and the rules on them are usually the result of the campground staff's years of experiences with campers of all sorts in that particular campground. They are designed to inform you of not only the most expedient and safest procedures for that campground, but also to guide you toward behaviors that allow other campers to have an equally pleasant camping experience. Although many rules found at campgrounds are quite similar, there are often major differences. Possibly the most important thing to note is the time of the evening designated as "quiet time." It may begin at 9 p.m. at one campground and 11 p.m. at another. If you have a dog you should pay particular attention to rules concerning leashes, areas where dogs are or aren't allowed, and rules about picking up after your dog. If a map of the campground is available you should note whether some roads are designated as one-way and be sure you always move your vehicle in the direction indicated. A map may also indicate which campsites can be reserved and which are readily available, first come, first served.

Some fliers include other useful information about such things as local hiking trails, popular attractions, and even local shopping. Some even offer coupons for local commercial enterprises; but even if no coupons are available, be sure to mention the campground's advertising when you shop at the places they advertise. Doing so can sometimes result in a discount, but may also indirectly help the campground.

Hang-tags, Dash Cards and Post Markers

When you register or self-register at a campground you will more than likely come away with some sort of card or other item intended to be used to indicate your paid occupancy of a campsite and probably the date of the end of your stay. This is a fairly important item and should be displayed appropriately. Many such markers are imprinted with a very condensed list of important information such as, quiet hours, time in which the running of generators is authorized, dog leash restrictions, and possibly the time the gates of the campground are locked. Often there is just too much to absorb during registration and this important information is overlooked. Try to remember to examine these tags or cards as you place them where they should be displayed. Displaying them, by the way, is very important. If the cards or markers are meant to be placed on a post then that should be done the moment you arrive at your campsite. Hang-tags - those cards designed to hang from your vehicle's rear-view mirror - should be attached as soon as they are received. (If you have more than one vehicle be sure to get a second tag.) When you park at your campsite you should always park so that your tag is clearly visible from the access road. These markers are used by campground employees for a variety of purposes, the most important of which is for your safety. Hang-tags help to ensure that no unauthorized people are in the campground.

Bathrooms/Showers/Facilities

It is good to know in advance what sort of facilities are available at your chosen destination. Some campgrounds, particularly state and federal campgrounds may furnish little more than a few scattered pit-toilets or port-a-johns.

Most campground bathrooms furnish toilet paper. In some places the paper furnished is the cheapest available and as such will tear off the moment you pull on it regardless of perforations or else it might be the roughest paper you have ever experienced. You might be fortunate enough to be at a more compassionate campground where reasonably soft and strong paper is supplied. Normally this paper is in the form of huge rolls that are locked within a transparent plastic dispenser. But sometimes there are multiple rolls that are designed so that when one roll is used up the next one is automatically made available. Unfortunately, this latter system only works if the paper rolls are properly and carefully installed, which isn't always the case. There are few things more frustrating than to be in need of toilet paper, to have it right where you can see it and yet you cannot access it. As a general rule it is best to bring your own just in case you need it.

Don't take it for granted that all campgrounds have shower facilities or even have hot water. Many state and federal campgrounds - especially the more rustic ones – might not have either of these. You may encounter campgrounds that have very few sources for drinking water and can often be at quite some distance from one another. Sometimes if showers are available you must pay for their use in much the same way as at a car wash. A quarter might purchase a certain number of minutes of shower time. It may also be that the shower will not become activated until a minimum number of quarters are deposited.

A useful backup to have on hand if neither water nor showers are likely to be available is a package or two of pre-moistened bath wipes. These are similar to the wipes used for cleaning babies except they are usually somewhat larger. Many are considerably thicker as well. Look for some that don't use alcohol. Even without alcohol some wipes feel quite cold when first you begin to use them. After a few moments, though, they become quite pleasant. If you are camping in an RV with electrical hookup you can microwave some brands of bath wipes so they won't feel quite so chilly. Read and follow the instructions on the package carefully.

Choosing A Campsite

An ideal campsite should be big enough. It should be located conveniently close to drinking water and bathrooms (where available) but far enough from potential sources of noise. The campsite should be within easy walking distance of those aspects of the campground that are of interest to the camper, such as a lake, a playground, or a hiking trail.

Most state or federally run campgrounds make use of a large contractor to handle camping reservations. Many such contractors are in charge of reservations for a great number of campgrounds. Because of this, their personnel usually are quite limited as to how much information they have available for a campsite's particular features. Although it is wonderfully convenient to reserve a campsite online, you may encounter problems because there could be certain important bits of information missing or unavailable.

Often all you are asked is whether you are tent camping or camping in an RV and the dates you have in mind. If you will be using an RV the next question might be its length. Beware that some older campgrounds are simply not set up to accommodate some of the longer RVs. The trees in some campsites can be problematic with regard to there being enough room for slide-outs. If you are tent camping you are rarely asked if your tent is big or small or even if you might be pitching more than one. It could be up to you to initiate that discussion. When viewing online you might get a glimpse of a map of the campground that may or may not be very accurate as to sizes of sites or distances from other features of the campground, such as bathrooms.

Websites do sometimes display photos of the campsites; but it is often difficult to get an idea of the slant or surroundings from a single, two-dimensional photo. For that reason, some campgrounds indicate the approximate slope of the sites and sometimes even the approach. Often the slope is expressed as a percentage. Without going into the mathematics of slope computation, let it be enough to know that the bigger the percentage number, the steeper the slope will be.

All too often I have seen the drama of someone in a two-wheel-drive pickup that has spewed gravel from increasingly deep divots as they attempted to back their 35-foot trailer up the 30% slope of their campsite's driveway. There have also been instances in which the campsite, itself, was just too slanted for comfortable tent camping or for RV set-up. Speaking with someone who has first-hand knowledge about a campsite is always advisable when possible. If you have never been to your chosen campground before, it is a good idea to phone the camp office directly in order to get clear answers to questions you may have about certain campsites or campground facilities. If heavy rain is in the forecast it may be wise to ask whether a particular site you have in mind is prone to drainage problems.

Something else to consider if you are tent camping is whether generators are allowed in your campground. If they are, will their noise be bothersome to you at the campsite you choose? To avoid that problem, check to see if there is a "generator free" zone. RVers should also be very aware of all campground regulations regarding generator use. Most campgrounds have strict limitations as to when and where generators are allowed to be run. Often the hours for generator use are for only 3- or 4-hour periods in morning and evening.

When selecting a campsite much depends upon what and how much equipment you plan to bring. Whether or not you have reserved a campsite it is likely that you must register as you arrive at the campground. If you discover that the site you selected is somehow inadequate, or if you do not have a reservation it is probable that the campground office staff will be able to point you toward a site that can accommodate your needs.

Where tent pads are clearly designated by implanted timbers or other markings you must cast a careful eye upon a potential campsite to see if your equipment is likely to fit. Campgrounds may have rules demanding that no tents may be set up anywhere other than on the designated tent pad. Be aware also that campgrounds' rules vary as to how many tents may occupy a site. In fact, some campgrounds stipulate that any tent or tent-like structure, including a screen tent or a small privacy tent can count as an additional tent. Rules can also govern how many campers may occupy a campsite. If you have a large family or wish to camp with a few friends, the total of which would put you over the stated limit, it won't do any harm to ask if there can be an exception made or if a "group camping" area is available, but such arrangements are best made far in advance. Group camping areas usually cost quite a lot more than regular campsites and often have limits for the minimum and maximum number of campers.

Another concept for consideration is location. Sure, nearly anyone would want the bathroom to be handy to their campsite, particularly if very small children are part of your camp. However, it is rarely a good idea to camp directly adjacent to a bathroom. People will almost invariably cut across or through your campsite on their way to the facilities. There can also be other reasons that don't appear on the websites.

We once camped near a beautiful. gurgling trout stream in a somewhat remote state park. The tent was up, campfire going, and since we had gotten an early start, we were almost ready for lunch. Then the breeze shifted slightly. Suddenly we were acutely aware of a horrible odor. Unknowingly, we had managed to choose a campsite within just a few yards of a pit toilet! Although there was a small path to it, the pit toilet was hidden from our view by some underbrush. Fortunately, there came a rainstorm followed by a far more favorable shift in the wind that remained for the rest of our (fortunately brief) stay. From that time forward you can bet we always made sure we knew our campsite's location in relation to that of the facilities.

Cellphones

In some campgrounds or other camping locations you may discover that obtaining enough signal strength to make use of your cellphone could be a real challenge. If you encounter that kind of difficulty and you have great need of keeping in touch with the outside world, it may be prudent to ask a campground representative or ranger if there are any particular spots nearby where a signal might more easily be found.

One campground I remember had only two small areas where cell signals could be received. Even then a lot depended upon the weather. If cellphone service is imperative because you are perpetually on call, you should discover any potential signal limitations before committing to a particular campground or camping spot.

On the subject of phones, it should be pointed out that it is important to have emergency contact numbers at hand or programmed into your phone. These can include the phone numbers (including after business hours numbers) for contacting a ranger, local law enforcement, campground management, and camp hosts.

Special Needs

Some campers require certain accommodations in order for their camping adventures to be all they should be. Many, if not all, state and national parks have done much to make these campers more comfortable. For instance, some campsites feature raised fire pits and specially extended picnic tables to make those things more accessible for people in wheelchairs. Many campgrounds have sites with electrical outlets available for recharging such things as power chairs, motorized wheelchairs, and for people who require the use of CPAP devices. If further accommodations are needed then the best recourse is to check with the campground office, a ranger, or a camp host for additional assistance.

CAMPING LIST

WHAT TO BRING WITH YOU:

I won't go into a lot of detail within these general categories because you will need to customize the list to suit your own needs and camping style, whether it is backpacking, car camping, or camping in a motorhome, etc.. There are many very detailed camping lists available on the internet, but you will never find a camping list that includes everything you might need for your particular camping adventure.

Particulars regarding many of the items that might fit into the categories listed here, are explained and described in later sections of this book.

Shelter

If you will be using a tent you will need to be sure you have all of the vital parts needed for it to do its job. Double-check tent poles, stakes, and tiedowns.

If you plan to use an RV you will need to check all of its systems to ensure all is in proper working order. Pay particular attention to tire pressure.

Bedding

Tent campers should air out your sleeping bags. Check inflatable mattresses for possible leaks. Think about what pillow(s) you will need.

RV campers should make sure there are sufficient sheets and blankets for all.

Check weather to be sure your crew will be warm enough and comfortable.

Lighting

Have fresh batteries or fuel for all lighting including spare mantles for your fueled lantern. Candles might be handy as backups. Be sure to have matches or lighters.

Stove

Make sure you have sufficient fuel for whatever kind of stove you use. Also be sure you have matches or lighters in case you would want a campfire.

Food and Drink

Plan your meals to ensure you have what will be needed. Bring more liquid refreshments than you estimate will be necessary. It is always better to have extra rather than not enough. If potable water will not be available you will need to bring enough for drinking as well as for cooking purposes.

Cooking and Eating

Cookware you will need is dependent upon your menu choices. Likewise, the cooking tools you bring should be in keeping with the menu. Also, you will require eating utensils, plates, cups, and whatever else you can picture as part of the eating scenario - napkins, for instance. A clean area for food preparation would also be helpful. Even an old plastic placemat could be useful.

Cleanup

You'll need somewhere to put your trash. You'll also want to have what you need to clean your cookware, cutlery, etc. and possibly a container in which to wash them.

Clothing and Footwear

Clothing choices should reflect the possible changes in weather as well as the expected activities. Spare clothing for unforeseen problems should be included. Footwear choices should reflect whatever activities you anticipate. Think also of something easy to slip into in case nature should call in the middle of the night.

Toiletries

While still at home, as you go through your daily routines of tooth brushing, hair grooming, body washing, and so on, consider what you will need to accomplish those tasks while camping or whether they will be necessary.

Tools

If you are not handy with tools you might not need many. However, sometimes equipment breaks or needs adjustment. At minimum, a good pocket multi-tool and a roll of duck tape should accompany any camping adventure. A few feet of parachute cord or 1/8-inch braided nylon rope can serve many purposes in a pinch.

Medications and First Aid

Plan to have enough of your daily medications to last for the entirety of your trip, plus a little extra, just in case. Also have at hand a first aid kit that is appropriate for your activities and complete enough to serve you and your companions.

EQUIPMENT

I have spent a lifetime accumulating thousands of dollars' worth of camping gear. Some of it I purchased out of necessity and some for trying out a new style of camping. Not all the gear lived up to expectations and some of it proved to be almost worthless. Gathering the right equipment for your camping needs is an ongoing process. Each camping experience can demonstrate a need for some small thing that could make future camping more comfortable, easier, or in some other way, nicer.

As a general rule regarding equipment: **always get the best you can afford.** But that rule is necessarily coupled with another one: **you usually get what you pay for.** Another consideration has to do with whether a piece of equipment is suited to the kind of camping you are planning as well as whether you have the capacity to transport that equipment to where you want it used. Most of all, ask yourself if it is truly a necessity for the camping trip you have in mind. It is so tempting to purchase stuff that really doesn't directly suit your needs.

Nonetheless, it seems that no matter how well outfitted you become there will always be some "perfect" thing you'll see in a catalog or else you'll see another camper using an "invaluable" item that they have had the wisdom to purchase. Naturally, you must have one! There have been some very wonderful innovations in camping equipment within the past fifty years or so and more are sure to come. If nothing else, much of camping equipment has become more compact and often of much lighter weight.

I often think of the immensely thick, heavy canvas umbrella tent and an accompanying canvas tarp my parents always lugged to campsites. I am unsure of the actual weight, but am reasonably certain that my father never attempted to lift both the folded tent and the tarp at the same time. Nowadays an unstaked tent - even with rainfly in place - usually can be picked up by one or two people and can be moved to a different location with complete ease.

It is entirely possible and even probable that you will not pack or make use of all of the equipment described in this section. Experience will teach you what is most vital to your particular style of camping.

Brands

If you are looking for particular brand endorsements, you'll find only a few of them specified here. I have my favorites; eventually you will develop your own if you don't already have them. If you talk to enough people who aren't trying to sell you something you will begin to recognize which brand names are most highly regarded. At the same time, you should bear in mind that a company might be especially outstanding in their manufacture of sportswear, for instance, but may be of dismal quality in their offering of tents.

The mega-outfitters, like most stores anywhere, cannot possibly stock every good or even great brand available. Your in-store choices are always limited by whatever deals the store's purchasing department was able to make and by how much space the store has to display the items. Nonetheless, it almost invariably proves best to actually lay eyes upon most products before purchasing. If at all possible, visit a variety of stores where you can examine the construction and quality of a number of manufacturers of an item. Then later, after having shopped around a bit you may decide to try an online source for your actual purchase. Sometimes the website of the very same store you visited could have a better price.

An exception here is if the item you want is sold at a reasonable price by a small, local store. It is usually well worth a slight price difference to support the local business, if for no other reason than for the personal service and advice most of them offer.

Tents

It has been my (sometimes unfortunate) experience that if you skimp on the cost of a good tent you will eventually suffer the consequences. Look carefully at a great number of tents. Catalogs or online photos can only tell you a few things. If there is a campground near where you live or even while you are camping elsewhere, it would probably be well worth the time to walk around and look at the various tents you see people using. It can be extremely useful to talk with other campers to get an idea of what pitfalls they have encountered with their tents. Ask them if they have used their tent very much. If it is still relatively new to them, then be suspicious of any accolades they may proffer. Some campers may like the size and shape of their tent; but have found problems with the zippers, or with how the windows open, or that the entry is awkward. Simply finding out what someone likes best or least about a particular tent can be instructive and useful.

Tent Style and Design

Consider also the design in terms of less than ideal weather. Is there a provision for cross-ventilation? This is an important consideration particularly on hot, sunny days. It can be absolutely vital when you have small children who require naps during the day. Can you enter the tent during a rainstorm without allowing a lot of rain into the tent? Is there any means, such as a vestibule, by which you can enter the tent without bringing in your muddy shoes or boots? If there are windows, could they be adequately sealed to prevent rain from entering? Very important on a list of potential questions is: Is there enough room for you to get dressed in it? Of course, this would be a moot point if there were no room for your extra clothing as well as for yourself and/or others. Anyone who has had to get dressed in a backpacker's tent has a good idea of how awkward it can be just to slip into a pair of pants.

Of course, much depends upon your camping needs. Camping with children may require a tent containing separate rooms. Or, if they are old enough, a separate tent might be just the thing. A tent that includes a screened dining area may suit your needs. If you plan to camp in cold and snowstorms you would likely need a much more wind-worthy tent than someone who plans only to camp in late spring and early summer. Consider what sort of weather conditions you might encounter. Know that a tent with broad, tall walls will capture wind and could even become airborne during the fiercer storms. A tent with inward-sloping walls may funnel rain toward window openings. For most campground campers, though, a good, three-season (spring, summer, fall) tent will be suitable.

Tent Construction

Construction of the tent is important. Your desires regarding weight and packed size can affect your choice of the fabric used to make the tent. A tent can be made of cotton (canvas), nylon, or other modern fabric. If you plan to do mostly car camping then weight is not usually much of an issue. But if you or a pack animal must carry your tent very far you would probably want to give much thought to the weight of your tent and how big of a bundle it is when packed.

Tubular, aluminum tent poles are sturdier than fiberglass ones and stand up to wear far better. The best thing about the aluminum poles besides their light weight is that, unlike fiberglass poles, they are highly unlikely to break.

Examine the seams of tents to check for quality. Even if you know next to nothing about sewing you will probably be able to spot poorly stitched seams.

Of particular note is the concept of how many people it sleeps. More often than not, manufacturers measure tent capacity as though people could be stacked side by side like cord wood. In reality, it might be good to think of capacity in terms of specifying for one or two more occupants than you picture being in your party. This will help you to allow for that bag of clothing or the small container of kids' toys or other such necessities.

A foyer or vestibule can prove invaluable during a rainstorm. At minimum it can allow enough room for muddy or sandy boots or shoes to be removed before entering the tent. If there is room for a folding chair, all the better. A chair can be extremely useful and helpful when boots or even when wet clothing needs to be removed. A vestibule large enough for a couple of small chairs can be great for allowing a dry spot from which to watch the storm.

Rainfly

One thing I have seen in campgrounds is that scores of campers make use of the ubiquitous blue, plastic tarp. Campers often rig tarps either to compensate for poor tent design with regard to protection from the rain or else as an attempt to keep the tent shaded enough for small children to sleep in at naptime. A good tent with a good rainfly should offer adequate protection from rain or the heat of bright sunlight except in the most extreme weather.

One of the reasons a full coverage rainfly or outer tent covering is needed is because of the way in which some tent fabrics repel rain. The cotton threads of canvas become swollen as they absorb water, pinching tighter the spaces between the threads. The trapped water creates a surface tension that prevents more water from penetrating. (This explains why a light spray of tiny droplets is sometimes felt inside a canvas tent at the start of a rainstorm but not after a short time.) Simply touching the canvas can interfere with the surface tension, creating an avenue by which water can penetrate the fabric. Before long, the leaking rainwater might wet the tent floor and possibly a sleeping bag as well. Learning to never touch the tent walls or roof during a rain is an important lesson for any tent camper. It is especially difficult yet important to teach young children this lesson.

Nylon tents are made waterproof by way of a polyurethane coating. Not all nylon tent fabrics are coated as thickly as others. Water resistance is graded on the ability to withstand pressure such as that caused by a heavy, pounding rain rather than a light sprinkle. Usually the rainfly of a nylon tent is made of a more moisture resistant grade of coating than is likely to be found in a tent. The rainfly's specially coated fabric is designed to withstand direct hits of raindrops instead of the glancing blows that might impact the sides of the tent at an angle. Even if the polyurethane coating of the fly might be enough to keep out the rain, the seams, flaps and zippers at the window and door openings might not. It pays to bear this in mind when selecting a tent as well as when applying sealant or other waterproofing. Many tents appear to be designed as though rain always falls straight down. It doesn't take much of a wind to blow rain under a window flap or through the door opening of a tent that isn't well protected. This is why I favor tents that feature a rainfly that extends all the way to the ground instead of the small, nearly useless, "weatherproof" patch that comes with many poorly designed tents.

There is a right way to install a rainfly. A good rainfly when properly mounted should be taut and should stand out and away from the surface of the tent. Some folks appear to believe that a rainfly is necessary only if foul weather is expected. Put it up anyway! A rainfly offers protection from the elements - including giving some respite from the heat of the sun. In fact, the shade of a rainfly can actually cause air movement, albeit just a little, when no breeze is present. An additional feature is that a full coverage rainfly can allow your tent to be ventilated despite harsh weather. Window flaps can remain furled when a good rainfly is in place. Ventilation, by the way, is important not only for comfort but also because it prevents the accumulation of moisture within the tent from exhaled air.

Tent Poles and Stakes

Poles

Probably the most important feature of a tent, besides protection from the elements, is the ease with which it can be erected. (Note that some pedants insist that a tent is always "pitched" rather than "set up," "put up," or "erected.") If you were to arrive at your campsite after dark would you really want to have to try to locate the 18-inch tent pole section that must slide into the orange sleeve nearest the third grommet from the left front of the tent - and to do all of this just to begin the process? Most of the better tent manufacturers have made erecting a tent fairly easy by connecting tent pole sections by way of elastic cords. But even with the aid of that innovation, putting up a tent – especially in the dark - can be daunting. This is one more reason why it is a good idea to practice once or twice with a new tent, or with one that hasn't been used recently, before you leave on your trip. You might also find it useful to label some of the parts with colored tape. For instance, the poles for the rainfly or for the vestibule could more easily be distinguished from the tent poles if this were done.

Somewhat new on the market are carbon fiber poles. The carbon fiber poles are said by users to be stronger than the aluminum ones. This is not often the case, though. Some of the carbon fiber poles sold for tent use are crafted from arrow stock, the strength of which is not designed for the lateral pull needed to support many tents. While the better carbon fiber poles might not splinter as easily as fiberglass poles (especially at low temperatures) and may also be very lightweight, carbon fiber poles are still a long way from general acceptance.

When pitching a tent in an area where bad weather can strike with little warning a tent should be completely set up, including rainfly and all guy ropes and stakes. If foul weather comes suddenly you then have a dry place to wait it out. Most good tents can withstand surprising amounts of wind and rain without collapse or damage so long as they are fully rigged according to the manufacturer's recommendations.

Stakes

Always stake your tent. Just as you can lift most tents off the ground easily, so too, can the wind. I have watched a high wind cause a nearly empty, unstaked tent to cartwheel for at least a hundred yards. Amazingly, that tent wasn't blown against some low branches or briers where it would have been shredded. However, the sleeping bag inside was completely soaked by the rain that accompanied the wind.

In solid or rocky ground planting tent stakes can be problematic and particularly so if you forget to bring a hammer. In a pinch, though, you can make use of a short piece of a small log. A rock can be used as a hammer but presents a problem. The rock needs to be heavy enough to be useful and yet small enough to grip. Gripping a rock while pounding with it will almost certainly put fingertips in harm's way. Be careful!

Remember also that tent stakes should always be slanted with their tops pointed away from the tent. This is to offer the most resistance to the pull of guy ropes or even that of the tent, itself.

Tent stakes are usually fairly inexpensive. The most commonly found stakes are made of plastic. Some are good and sturdy; some are horrid and brittle. It is difficult sometimes to decide which ones might be most adequate. Usually, you get what you pay for. The same axiom holds true for metal stakes. Some will bend the moment you attempt to make use of them. Others seem to be nearly indestructible. In either case it is a good idea to have extras on hand because tent stakes have a way of getting bent, lost, or left behind. In most campgrounds I have seen, at least the ones without camp stores, the camp office or camp host keeps a small collection of tent stakes that have been left by previous campers. If you happen to discover that you are missing a stake or two, just ask.

In sand or in extremely loose soil what is sometimes called a "dead man" can be used in place of a stake. Usually a "dead man" consists of a log or large stone to which the tent's tiedown is attached before the "dead man" is buried. A log is normally positioned so it is parallel to the ground's surface and perpendicular to the pull of the rope or guy. A stone is situated so it's broadest face is toward the line of pull. In sand I have also used a square of strong cloth or canvas, with its corners tied like a parachute, attached to the tiedown and then buried. The parachute can also be loaded with small stones. Some stores sell versions of these "sand parachutes."

Tent Footprints

Rather than the waterproof "bathtub" floor and lower wall coating often found in less expensive tents, some tents come with a "footprint" or tailored, waterproof ground cloth upon which to place the tent. Other tents have footprints that are sold separately.

Footprints have two functions. First, they aide in keeping small stones or twigs from puncturing the floor of your tent. Second, they help to prevent water and ground moisture from seeping up through the floor of your tent. If you purchase a particularly eccentrically shaped tent then it is probably best to purchase the "footprint" to match it. Also, some footprints have grommets specially placed on them to accommodate the ends of the poles of a particular tent, making them all the more valuable to the tent owner. However, a serviceable ground cloth or custom "footprint" can be made fairly easily.

Search the paint department of your hardware or home improvement store for a thick, (0.6 to 1 Mil is thick) usually clear, plastic tarp or drop cloth that is a little bigger than the base of your tent. Set up your tent (unstaked) in the back yard or elsewhere, having smoothly spread the tarp beneath it. After you have insured that the tarp has been made as flat as possible and using a marking pen, outline the base of the tent, leaving about an inch or so margin to prevent accidentally marking the tent. Remove the tarp and begin cutting it with scissors, following your markings but cutting inside the marks by about two inches. The finished product should now be a custom-made ground cloth for your tent. If you can find a ready-made thick ground cloth of a size that is quite similar to that of your tent, all the better. Just remember when you have it under your tent to fold under any excess that might stick out in order to prevent funneling rainwater runoff under your tent. (Please also see the section on RAIN and HARSH WEATHER.)

Where to Pitch Your Tent

In campgrounds you sometimes have little choice as to where to place your tent. You are somewhat limited by the size of the area the campground designated for it. If possible, though, your tent should sit so as to take best advantage of whatever direct sunlight there is. In this way the sun can dry off the morning dew or any rain that may have fallen. The location of your tent near the protection of trees may be of importance with regard to high winds. However, the tent should have few branches directly overhead except for the sake of a little shade. One of the problems with having tree branches, especially rotten ones, above your tent is the possibility of their falling onto it. Another is what I call, "second rain" which is the seemingly endless dripping from the leaves long after a rainstorm has passed. For safety the tent also should, if possible, be situated where it is at least 15 feet from the campfire. If you are camping in a much more primitive setting on a hillside near a lake or stream it would be wise to pitch your tent 10 to 20 feet uphill from the bank. In this way your tent will be less likely to become saturated by a morning fog coming off the water.

It also pays to give some thought as to what direction the tent's main opening should face. What is most convenient for your needs? When you are setting up camp or later, emptying your tent, would it be easier if the tent's entry faces your vehicle? After a hot summer's night when you have the entry fly open will you want the morning sun to wake you as it rises? From which direction is foul weather likely to come?

There is no single answer to fit all situations, but being able to readily identify which edge of the tent holds the entrance is important. As you unfold your tent it is sometimes difficult to figure out which way is "front." You can solve this problem by tying a brightly colored ribbon to one or more of the stake loops or grommets usually found at either side of the entry.

Something to bear in mind as well when pitching a tent on a slope is where you envision the occupants to sleep such that their heads will be on the uphill side. It can be quite uncomfortable to try to sleep when it feels as though all of your blood is rushing to your head! Also, you should consider potential water drainage issues in case of rain. Is a flood of water likely to take a shortcut through your tent? (Be aware that trenching to divert groundwater flow is prohibited almost universally.)

Bedding

Sleeping Bags

The main consideration with sleeping bags is to get one that will keep you in comfort during the coldest weather you are likely to encounter when you are camping. A bag that is rated for comfort at forty degrees below zero will likely be far too warm for you if most of your camping weather will range between fifty and ninety degrees above zero (Fahrenheit.) However, if your camping adventures will put you in extremely low temperatures, your bag should reflect the capacity for comfort at about ten to twenty degrees lower than the lowest temperature you expect to encounter. If the expected weather falls into the all-too-warm or way-too-humid range, you can just use your sleeping bag as an additional mattress to sleep upon.

The shape of your sleeping bag is certainly a matter of choice for the most part. However, it is a rule of thumb that the more closely a bag fits you the warmer it will keep you. In warmer weather you may prefer the roominess of a rectangular bag.

Some people prefer to bring bed linens along when they camp. Sheets can be great for avoiding sweating in or on your sleeping bag on hot nights. Sometimes it might just feel like a bit of luxury to sleep between some crisp sheets after a hard day of camping. You can simplify using a sheet in a single, rectangular sleeping bag by folding a top sheet of sufficient size in half lengthwise and then sewing a hem along the bottom edge to match the length of your bag. This liner can then be inserted into the bag and is unlikely to interfere with the sleeping bag's zipper. Doing this is probably much less expensive than buying a commercially sold sleeping bag liner.

Mattresses and Pillows

It is said that if you are tired enough you can sleep standing up. But short of that you might require a bit of something comfortable between you and the ground. Needs and degrees of comfort vary greatly as do weight and space limitations.

Some people are dead set against inflatable mattresses because, they argue, the air space within the mattresses may never become warm enough for comfort. Others find no issues with air mattresses at all and especially appreciate the self-inflating mattresses. Let me interject here that it is no fun at all after a long day at the end of which camp had to be made on rocky ground and then to discover that the air mattress or self-inflating mattress won't hold air.

If you choose to use an air mattress you might do well to bring along a backup. Cheap, plastic mattresses as are sold for use in swimming pools can serve well in a pinch. A foam pad might also make for a good backup. Many backpackers favor the foam pads because the pads weigh so little. Foam pads are normally lighter and are deemed to be more dependable than inflatable mattresses. Most foam pads, however, in order to reduce their bulk, are necessarily thin and as such offer only marginally good protection from the hard ground. But again, if you're tired enough ....

Some inflatable mattresses include an attached pillow or else a raised area that might serve as a pillow. You'll probably prefer the attached pillow because it is usually separately arranged so its inflation can be adjusted to suit your preference. On the other hand, you might wish to just have a flat mattress and supply your own pillow. Depending upon the kind of camping you choose, a full-size pillow from home, despite its bulk, might best suit your needs. However, your local backpackers' outfitter can show you some small, comfortable, and quite compactable pillows if space is an issue.

Lighting

Lanterns

Camping with my parents nearly always meant evenings lit by and accompanied by the whooshing sound of a Coleman liquid gas lantern. The whooshing is still often part of many people's camping experience, but in many cases modern lanterns are fueled by propane instead of the special liquid fuel or the "white gas" my folks used. On most of the newer models virtually the same wicks (properly referred to as mantels) are used as those of the older style lanterns. Mantels become quite fragile upon burning and so a supply of replacement mantels should always be available. I usually tape a couple to the bottom of the lantern or to the propane tank. The procedure for dismantling the lantern and replacing the mantel is a bit tricky and should therefore best be practiced at home. You're probably going to want to start out with a fresh mantle anyway.

There are some campers who prefer to use kerosene lanterns or even tiki torches. The light from these is of a very pleasant color and the lanterns barely flicker when the wind blows. When the wicks are properly trimmed neither the lanterns nor the torches smoke very much. A reservoir full of the very refined, "smokeless" fuels now recommended for these will last for quite some time.

For many other campers the preference is to make use of battery-powered, LED lighting. LED lamps are wonderfully efficient, boasting of hundreds of hours of useful battery life in some instances. LED lanterns, though they offer a surprising amount of light, deliver a blue-white glow that is completely lacking in visual warmth, but they get the job done.

My favorite lantern is a small, candle-powered wonder that I discovered when I was outfitting for a backpacking trip. The lantern is compact. It is not much bigger than a juice glass and burns short "plumbers' candles" which can last for more than eight hours each. The lantern is wind-proof and is generally weatherproof as well. It supplies a surprising amount of warm and pleasant light for its size. Although this candle lantern is not expensive, there is an extremely cheap version of it that can be found at some stores and should be avoided because it doesn't perform nearly as well. The one I admire is called the UCO Original Collapsible Candle Lantern.

Whatever type of lantern you might choose may have a built-in pitfall or two. Liquid fuel-type lanterns require a supply liquid fuel. Propane lanterns require spare propane tanks. Battery-powered lanterns require spare batteries. Candle lanterns require spare candles. If space or convenience are issues, then your choice of lighting should include considering what else they require.

Flashlights

It is difficult for me to imagine having too many flashlights. When the need arises I want one close at hand and where I can easily access it. The more there are available, the more this is possible.

Flashlights come in numerous lengths and configurations and deliver various amounts of light. Some can even be transformed into artificial candles. What is also important is the size. The main drawback to having a variety of sizes of flashlights in the camp is the need, in most cases, for a matching variety of spare batteries. Although the batteries in LED flashlights last for amazing amounts of time, they do eventually need replacement. Certainly, the more traditional kinds of flashlights share that need. I find it particularly practical to make use of flashlights, most of which require the same size of battery.

In recent years there has been an upswing of the use of headlamps and hat lamps by many campers. At times it is awkward to try to hold a flashlight while performing any number of tasks. This is where the headlamps and hat lights excel. But while these hat lamps and headlamps provide illumination of anything toward which the user points his head, this same feature can be a problem. The beams of the headlamps and hat lamps can be a glaring nuisance (pun intended) to anyone who attempts to look the wearer in the eye during conversation. To avoid temporarily blinding others, the lamp beams should be aimed to shine somewhat beneath, above, or to one side of the center line of the wearer's field of vision.

Camp Stoves

If a single-burner stove will allow you to accomplish your cooking goals then that is what you should bring. If you need to have two or more burners going simultaneously then you should give careful consideration when purchasing a stove as to whether the burners are of sufficient size and are spread far enough apart to accommodate the pots or pans you will use. The propane-fueled stoves and liquid-fueled stoves carry with them some of the pitfalls mentioned in the section on lanterns as to which kind of fuels you want to deal with. Also, your choice of fuels for your stove may rightly be influenced by whether you can use the same fuel for your lanterns.

Something to consider if you think you don't have any need for a camp stove is that a steady rain can squelch any plans for cooking over a campfire. Having a camp stove for a back-up can save the day if you have a sheltered area in which to use it.

The best camp stove in the world will be of no use to you whatsoever and can even be dangerous if you don't know how to properly light it. Years ago, I happened to encounter a camper who had a liquid-fueled camp stove he had never before used. The man had spent quite a while attempting to light a burner without results. The level of his frustration was proportional to the pile of spent matches on his picnic table. Having had much previous experience with an identical stove I asked if I could be of help. He explained that he had pumped the plunger many, many times; but he was still unable to get the fuel pressurized enough. My suspicions about the basis for the problem caused me to ask if I could watch one more attempt. Again, he pumped the plunger over and over and again he had no pressure. I took a turn at it. I showed him that there was a little trick to pressurizing the tank. I showed him the little hole in the top of the plunger that needed to be covered each time the plunger was depressed and released as the plunger was pulled back. After I pumped it a few times, he was able to light the burner at last.

The proper use of some camping equipment is not necessarily easy to figure out even with printed instructions at hand. For that reason, in order to avoid a few problems, any new equipment should be assembled and used before it is taken into the field.

Clothing and Towels

What to wear?

Weather has everything to do with the selection of clothing to bring for camping. If you consider nothing else, plan for foul weather. Your local weather forecast may have little to do with what will be happening in your mountain getaway. At the very least, plan for rain. The weather in many of the out-of-the-way places where you may plan to camp can undergo rapid changes, including sudden drops or increases in temperature. True, sometimes you'll bring items with you for which the need doesn't arise; but it is far better to have a jacket or raincoat when you need it than to suffer cold and/or wetness needlessly.

Some of the cheaper rain jackets and pants are great for keeping rain off, but tend to seal body warmth and particularly perspiration inside. There are rain suits now made of "miracle fabrics" that keep rain out but also allow perspiration to escape. Unfortunately, these fine garments are quite expensive; but well worth the expense when it comes to comfort.

Rain ponchos are in many ways great to have. They keep out most of the rain (except around the neck hole) and certainly allow plenty of ventilation. Ponchos pack very nicely and so don't take up a lot of space. The only downside I have ever experienced was when cooking over an open fire. It is quite difficult to accomplish campfire cooking while wearing a poncho and worrying about becoming a human torch.

Planning your clothing so that layering is possible can be quite useful as the weather warms or the temperature drops. Layering allows you to put on to or to remove however much clothing the temperature might dictate.

Opinions vary radically as to what kind of fabric works best for clothing in the outdoors. Some say that wool is best and it may be true for many situations. Others say that cotton clothing should be strictly avoided because it absorbs water too easily and likewise is difficult to dry. There are also advocates of the more modern fabrics, some of which are reputed to wick away moisture. In all likelihood, barring an allergy to wool, nearly any fabric you choose might possibly suit your needs.

Much depends upon the activities you plan, what weather you might encounter, and the duration of your camping adventure. If the activities you plan could involve getting your clothing extremely dirty and/or wet, then easily washed, quickly drying fabrics may be your best choice. If cold, wet weather or even snowstorms might be in the picture then you would probably do well to have clothing available made of wool or a wool blend, that would keep you at least somewhat warm even when it is wet. If you are just camping for an overnight, then it may hardly matter what you wear so long as you bring a spare, complete change of clothing. If you are camping for much more than a day or so then whether you can bring multiple changes of clothing or else have clothing you can easily wash and dry, might be worth consideration when planning your attire.

NOTE: *When planning clothing, never dress your small children in camouflage. Imagine for a moment that the child somehow wanders away from your campsite. How difficult would he/she be to find? Were the problem to become serious, consider this: Children are often frightened by searchers and have been known to hide from them. Wouldn't you want your child to be spotted easily? White or bright colors are best for numerous reasons. Besides being easier to see, the lighter colors are reputed to attract fewer flying insect pests.*

Towels and Washcloths

Some thought should be directed toward towels, whether beach towels, bath towels, or hand towels. Whatever kind is used at all is likely to be temporarily rendered unsuitable for further use until it is once again dry. It is because of the drying factor that there is much wisdom in having some cheap, much-less-than-plush towels for camping. Luxuriously soft and pleasant as plush towels may be, they simply will not dry readily. The far less fancy, utilitarian towels found at the bargain shops are much better suited to overnight drying. If, on the other hand, you are just planning an overnight camping trip then this sort of thing may not be as much of an issue. In any case, don't forget to pack a large plastic bag in which to contain the damp towels or clothing when it comes time to pack up and head for home.

Many stores that sell camping supplies offer some very lightweight and compact towels that appear to be made of compressed paper fibers. They are wonderfully absorbent and dry relatively quickly. Most hold up well enough for at least one reuse. (See also the section on Bathrooms/Showers/Facilities.)

Potable Water

Just like almost everyone else I had seen the many movies in which the main character pauses at a mountain stream and bends down to drink the water there. One of the very first times I camped near a lovely, gurgling brook I decided that I needed to duplicate that experience. The clarity of the water just below a small waterfall was such that I could see the bottom of a pool that was at least four feet deep. The water was so cold and refreshing! I satisfied my thirst and then walked upstream just twenty feet or so. It was there that I saw where the delicious water poured over a deer carcass lying crosswise to the flow. I doubt I need to spell out the moral of this story. I certainly learned a valuable lesson!

If drinkable water is not available at the area you have chosen for camping, you will almost certainly need to bring it with you. Sure, you will likely give a lot of thought to having soft drinks, fruit juices, and such, but don't forget that you will need potable water for cooking, for teeth brushing, as well as for drinking.

In areas where potable water is unlikely to be obtainable you might need to consider having the means for filtering and purifying whatever water will be available. Your local backpacking supply store will probably be your best resource for learning the best processes and equipment for the purpose. Filters capable of removing any particles larger than .05 microns would be advised.

Bringing water that has been minimally filtered (poured through a tee-shirt or other cloth) to a rolling boil for at least a minute (and some sources would even have you to boil it for twenty minutes) usually results in flat-tasting water. The flavor seems to improve after the boiled water sits for a few minutes. You can improve the water a little by pouring it back and forth between two containers.

Everyone I have ever spoken with about the use of tablets to purify minimally filtered water has said the result tasted terrible. Also, because of the iodine involved, this is truly a last resort.

Beer, Wine, and Booze

Regulations vary greatly among camping areas. Be sure you know what restrictions, if any, apply to the place where you intend to camp. Some campgrounds prohibit the use of any and all alcoholic beverages. Other camping areas are okay with alcoholic drinks so long as the drinking is done discretely. It is rather odd that such drinking is permitted so long as the bottles or cans are not readily visible, but those are the rules in some places. Yet in many other locations there are no limitations at all on alcoholic beverages.

Perhaps it is worth pointing out to recreational vehicle owners that in some states your motorhome is, for legal purposes, considered to be your domicile. As such you are entitled to drink whatever you please within your motorhome, no matter how temporary it may be. However, laws differ greatly from state to state and in some locales, they differ from county to county. If drinking alcoholic beverages is important to you, you should be aware of any local restrictions.

Toiletries

Prior to your camping trip you will need to consider which toiletries you will require. While at home, as you go through your daily routines of tooth brushing, hair grooming, body washing, and so on, consider what you will need to accomplish those tasks while camping. If you will be camping where a bathhouse is available you will need to have an appropriate container in which to carry your toiletries. Such a container is handy anyway for keeping all of your stuff in one place.

You might discover that you do not have access to electrical outlets to plug in electric shavers, hairdryers, and such. Some campers may decide to forgo shaving or else switch to shaving with a razor. Often a scarf or hat can come to the rescue of unruly hair. Some folks may be surprised to know there are rechargeable hairdryers and butane-powered curling irons to be had for camping use. These can be especially helpful for use in recreational vehicles where electrical power is somewhat limited.

Among the many necessities of camping is toilet paper. It is good to have some idea as to how much toilet paper you and your crew might use per day in order to be sure you bring enough. Toilet paper that is designed for septic system and/or RV use will suit most needs, particularly when camping where there are no bathrooms.

Anyplace you might be camping where bathrooms are not available as well as in some places where there are bathrooms on hand, you should be prepared to perform a number of hygiene activities away from camp. Remember that some animals, including bears, may be attracted by the scent of toothpaste or mouthwash when spat onto the ground.

Some thought also should be given to the awkwardness of brushing your teeth while trying to unscrew the cap of a water bottle to rinse your mouth.

In wilderness areas defecation and urination should also be done away from camp as well as at least a hundred feet away from streams, rivers, and lakes. All solid excretions should be buried along with any toilet paper you might use. Backpacker supply stores and even some "big box stores" sell lightweight trowels that are designed for digging what some people call "cat holes" for burying waste. If you make use of bathroom wipes, know that not all are biodegradable; those that aren't must be packed out for later proper disposal.

Sanitary napkins can be extremely useful not only for their intended purpose but also to cover bleeding wounds when necessary. Proper disposal of all used sanitary napkins is very important because the scent of blood could attract animals.

Makeup items, lipstick, lip gloss, and some cosmetic wipes may contain scented lotions or oils that can smell like food to skunks, raccoons, and bears. When wilderness camping you should be prepared to pack out any disposables that aren't biodegradable and to keep cosmetics, hand lotions, after-shave, and perfumes away from camp.

Some authorities recommend keeping food and other animal-attractants as much as a hundred yards away from camp. I would say a rule of thumb might be to ask yourself how close to camp would you want any of those animals?

Rope, Cord, String, Wire, and Tape

Having a few lengths of various kinds of rope available can often prove handy. The same holds true for having some cord, heavy string, tape, and possibly even some wire.

Rope of various thicknesses can be used for tasks such as creating a clothesline, for hanging a tarp, or even for an impromptu tug-of-war.

Cord is handy for tying down tent corners or for hanging small items to dry. A loop of cord placed around the top of a tent stake is great for pulling a stubborn stake from the ground.

If an ax handle shows signs of splitting or needs reinforcing, a few turns around it with some string will probably do the job. String might also be used as a temporary shoelace or to close a cloth bag.

If a tent pole should happen to break, an emergency repair might be made by way of some tight windings of thin, copper or stainless-steel wire.

A broken wire for an RVs taillight likely can be fixed with some electrician's tape. The innumerable uses for duck tape (also called duct tape) are legendary.

One item I find particularly helpful to have is a roll of brightly colored, vinyl tape of the kind surveyors use and commonly known as flagging tape. Flagging tape is non-adhesive. You can find flagging tape at a hardware store but may also encounter it among equipment used by hunters. The tape can be used to mark trails - especially if you need to wander off the more commonly used trails. (Just be sure that when you backtrack you remove the markers.)

Recently a biodegradable version of flagging tape became available. I haven't yet tried it, but some reviewers describe it as being somewhat like crepe paper in consistency and currently is not as brightly colored as the extruded plastic tape. The diminished brightness of color could limit its effectiveness for marking trails, but the tape's biodegradability could preclude the necessity for having to remove it.

I also use the tape to mark long lengths of rope or tiedowns as well as other obstacles that might be hazardous to someone wandering around camp at night with just a flashlight. Another use for the eye-catching tape to mark items such as an ax, hammer, or digging tool that might get set down somewhere it could become less than obvious.

Hand Tools

Besides an ax and saw (as discussed in the section on Cutting and Splitting of Firewood) there are some other hand tools that are good to have on hand when camping. A "dead blow" hammer is quite helpful when tent stakes must be driven into packed or rocky soil. Two screwdrivers, medium-sized and of both straight-blade and Phillips types, may be needed to tighten a screw on a piece of your equipment. Slip-joint pliers or medium-sized channel-lock pliers can help you out in a pinch, especially if you have misplaced the removable handle of a cooking pot. Needle-nose pliers can also be handy for manipulating very small items as well as for cutting wire with the built-in side-cutters found on most needle-nose pliers A small, military-style, folding shovel is great for rearranging the coals for cooking on a campfire. An edge of one of the sturdier of these shovels can be sharpened to make the shovel useful as an ax of sorts or for splitting kindling.

There's also a lot to be said for some of the pocket multi-tools that have gone far beyond the Swiss army knife in usefulness. Of course, the Swiss army knife still has its place among useful items. A simple, two-bladed Barlow knife can also be handy for many purposes.

First Aid Kit and Medications

A brief look at the wares of your local pharmacy or online store will reveal that there are first aid kits made for various activities and locations. If you are camping with your family there are some kits made to fill that need. If you plan to do some hiking, you'll find much more compact kits made especially for that purpose. Your doctor might be able to recommend a particular kit or can give you a list of the minimum items your kit should include. Consulting with your doctor can be particularly important if you have allergies or are especially sensitive to certain things you might encounter when camping. Be sure to mention to your doctor the area in which you intend to camp. It may affect which items your doctor might recommend.

When you look for a good first aid kit you will probably find that more isn't necessarily better. One kit may offer more pieces than another, but you might discover that the additional pieces consist of little more than a few more small adhesive bandages or more aspirins.

Most first aid kits come with instruction booklets. Read the booklet so you will have a better idea of what to do if a minor medical problem arises. You really don't want to need to take the time to read the manual during an emergency.

If you have allergies you should be sure to bring enough remedy for any anticipated need. This is particularly true of allergies for which an EpiPen or other epinephrine auto-injector could be needed.

If you carry an auto-injector make sure others with you know its whereabouts and know how to administer it properly.

Be sure to bring with you enough of any medicines you or your children would need to take regularly each day of your camping adventure plus an extra day's worth just in case. When camping it is very easy to lose track of time and miss a dose. This is especially true for children who often will become so involved with an activity that any notion of time slips away. Be sure to have checked with your or their doctor so you know what to do if a dose is missed.

In all likelihood you and whoever you bring with you will probably be exposed to more sun than usual. Be sure to bring some good sunblock with you. If you bring it, be sure to use it.

A problem that plagues a lot of campers is constipation. When camping you usually are much more active than in your daily life elsewhere. However, you might neglect to drink enough water to compensate for what is lost through sweating. The lack of sufficient water, along with what are probably different foods than you normally consume, can bring about problems in your bowels. My suggestion is that you force yourself to drink more water and encourage your campmates to do the same.

If the consumption of more water doesn't produce the desired effect then you might be glad that you included some stool softeners and/or laxatives among your medical supplies.

Be sure your first aid kit includes a good set of tweezers for removing thorns or splinters or even ticks. Be aware that some first aid kits contain items that appear to be tweezers but are actually more like forceps and so are virtually useless as tweezers. Also, recent advice for tick removal recommends that you cut a fine slit in the edge of an ID or credit card then slide the card's slit under the body of the tick so that it entraps the tick's head and then slowly lift with a gentle but firm motion.

A fine sewing needle could also be helpful for removing splinters. A small but good scissors is useful for cutting gauze and a surprising number of other tasks. Sometimes even one of the most basic of magnifying glasses can be of great help in a variety of situations. A clean pair of needle-nose pliers are not usually considered to be part of a first aid kit. However, they can be vital equipment when removing some kinds of cactus needles or porcupine spines. (Please also see the notes on ANAPHALACTIC SHOCK in the section on GENERAL SAFETY.)

Pots and Pans, Etc.

When you contemplate your needs, you should mentally walk yourself through your meal plans to ensure that you have all of the cookware you require and that all of it is of sufficient size for your needs.

Some people prefer to have a separate set of cookware for camping. This is particularly true of those who enjoy cooking over a campfire and don't relish the idea of having their household set of pots and pans blackened with soot. (Some say that a light coating of soap on the outside of pans will simplify soot removal.) Also, having a set of cookware already designated for camping can preclude some extra packing and planning. Cookware especially designed for camping is usually lightweight and compact. Often pots and pans will nest within one another and are constructed so that a single handle can be attached to any of them. I strongly urge you to purchase an additional detachable handle not only so you can manipulate more than one pot or pan at a time, but particularly so that you'll have a spare in case one goes missing. (Just don't keep both in the same location.) Many camp cook sets are specially coated to make cleanup much easier.

For some folks a large, cast iron skillet is all that is needed. A cast iron skillet is versatile in that it can be used just as easily on a camp stove as over a campfire. Cleanup of a seasoned cast iron skillet is also extremely easy, requiring no soap and little if any water because in most instances, a properly seasoned cast iron pan can be wiped out with a paper towel. (Particularly stubborn stuck-on food can be removed by scrubbing lightly with coarse salt.) This is also true of a Dutch oven - another cooking vessel preferred by many campers. Cast ironware is, of course, heavy. Many people don't like the added packing weight. Others have some difficulty lifting cast iron cookware while cooking and prefer the lightweight and more compact cookware.

Cutlery, Food Preparation, Eating Utensils, and Cleanup

Knives

When I cook at home, I have one knife in particular that I almost invariably reach for. It is a relatively straight-bladed, non-serrated one that is smaller than a chef's knife; yet it is larger than a steak knife. You may have a favorite "go-to" knife. For most camp cooking tasks, a single, sharp knife will serve very well. If you possess a clone of your favorite knife or can purchase one that is similar, then that is what you should bring along when camping. Occasionally, a small paring knife may be handy to have as well. Of course, if you plan to serve steaks then perhaps some additional knives could be needed, but the cutting necessary for most other foods can usually be accomplished with some of the sturdier of the disposable knives. Knives are of little use if they are not kept sharp. It is best to check your camping knives at the start of each camping season or more often to ensure that they are sharp.

Selecting Utensils for Food Preparation, Eating, and Cleanup

When outfitting a camping kitchen, you should try to pare down your implements to just a few. The fewer you bring, the fewer you must keep track of and clean after using. You must ask yourself whether you really see a need to bring your matched set of wooden spoons of various sizes or will a single, medium-sized spoon be adequate for most situations? Will an eggbeater really be necessary or can you accomplish the cooking tasks you have planned with a "granny fork?" On the other hand, there are some kitchen tools such as can openers which are very hard to do without.

In order to decide what utensils to bring you must have a fairly clear idea of what foods you will be preparing and possibly how many meals will be consumed. Once a menu has been planned you should try to picture every single step that would be involved from the moment you begin the meal preparation to the moment you and your bunch sit down to eat it. In the following long and tediously detailed example, let's say you decided to start off your first full day of camping with some sliced fruit, scrambled eggs, sausage patties, and biscuits. You will need to decide upon the best order in which to prepare the meal. Here is what might be needed or involved:

- You will need a clean surface of sufficient height upon which to prepare the food and a burner or two to cook upon or else a campfire with a cooking grate. Perhaps a picnic table or a folding table will be of the right height and a portion of a smooth, plastic tablecloth will serve as a clean surface. (Be aware that many campgrounds prohibit the use of camp stoves on their picnic tables. Also be sure that if you use a camp stove or burner that it is sufficiently distant from any plastic tablecloth.)

- To ensure your prep surface is clean enough you might want to bring some disinfectant kitchen wipes or some disinfecting liquid with which to clean it.

- You might need a vegetable peeler and/or paring knife for the next step.

- You may also need some small bowls or a serving bowl for the next step.

- Peel and slice the fruit, placing the slices in small bowls or in a single, large serving bowl. Where are you going to put the peelings?

- You will need a container or trash bag for the peelings and other trash from the meal preparation. (Please see the section on Campfires and Trash.)
- You will need to have a skillet large enough to hold, at one time or another, the quantity of eggs, number of sausage patties and possibly the number of biscuits that are required.
- If you plan to break the eggs into a bowl or other container prior to cooking then you will need a bowl or container for the purpose.
- Or you can break the eggs into a large plastic baggie (for which you will need to have that baggie.)
- You will need some salt and pepper to season the eggs. You may also wish to add a splash of milk or cream to the eggs. Mix the egg mixture until relatively smooth.
- If you are using a bowl you will need a mixing utensil such as a fork or spoon.
- If you choose to use a plastic bag you can simply squish the bag repeatedly until all is well mixed. If you are using a plastic baggie that zips then you should zip it closed.
- If the baggie doesn't zip you will need to have a twist tie or bag clamp.
- Set the mixture aside.
- If you are preparing the biscuits from a mix you have brought then you will need a second container big enough in which to do the mixing.
- If you use a bowl you may also need a mixing utensil that is strong enough for the purpose.
- You might also need to have brought some milk for the next step.
- Perhaps you created your own pre-mix or purchased one and stored or repackaged the loose mixture in a large plastic

baggie. If you did this then you could simply add some water or milk to the baggie and squish the mixture until it is of the desired consistency, ignoring lumps smaller than a pea.

- If you are using a bowl then stir the mixture to which you have added the liquid only until barely mixed, ignoring small lumps. Form bits of the dough into ½ inch thick rounds that are 2-3 inches in diameter. On the other hand, you may have bought one or more of the ready-to-bake biscuit rolls or even brought some pre-made, frozen biscuits which by now are likely to be at least partially thawed.
- If your recipe requires pre-greasing the cooking pan then you will need some cooking oil, or shortening for that purpose. (Butter may not be suitable for this due to the temperature and the length of cooking time required.)
- Preheat the skillet over a medium heat. Place the formed biscuits in the skillet, spreading them far enough apart that they do not touch. Fry the biscuits until golden brown on the bottom. If using frozen biscuits cook the first side until halfway heated. Monitor the heat carefully to prevent scorching. You may need to reposition some of the dough rounds to ensure they all brown at more or less the same rate.
- You will need a spatula with which to check and then later to turn the biscuits.
- Fry the other sides until done.
- You will need some paper towels and a kitchen towel or aluminum foil for the next step.
- Wrap the finished biscuits in paper towels and a kitchen towel to keep them warm or wrap them loosely in aluminum foil and set the foil package just near enough to the campfire (if you have one) to keep the contents warm. Turn that package 180 degrees from time to time to warm the biscuits more evenly.
- If you have brought a roll of breakfast sausage you'll need a clean cutting surface upon which to slice the roll into patties. If you have brought already-sliced patties you can skip this step.

- Place the sausage patties into the skillet and brown both sides until they are thoroughly cooked.

- You will need plates or a serving plate for the next step. It is your choice as to whether or not you want to use paper plates or some that will require washing.

- Place cooked sausages onto individual plates or a serving plate.

- If necessary, drain off excess grease from the sausage patties or absorb it with a paper towel. If draining the excess grease, you will need a receptacle to put it in either to discard it or to reserve the grease for a different purpose.

- Now add the beaten or mixed eggs to the skillet.

- I prefer to use a large, stainless spoon with which to scrape the eggs from the bottom of the pan occasionally as they cook. You may wish to use the spatula you have already been using or perhaps a different implement that you will have brought.

- You will probably want to have butter to serve with the biscuits. Or perhaps some honey or jelly might be needed. You may have kept a few serving packets of these latter two items that weren't used when you ate breakfast at a restaurant a few weeks before.

- You will need enough forks and knives in order for the food to be consumed. Whether to use stainless or disposable plastic-ware should be considered during planning. If plasticware is your choice you may give some thought to purchasing some of the more biodegradable ones that are made from cornstarch.

- If liquids such as milk or coffee are to accompany the meal then cups suited to the purpose should be at hand. (See how to make "camp coffee" in the section on CAMP COOKING.)

- Did everyone get a napkin? (Paper towels will do in a pinch.)

- Once the meal is over you will need to have some dish soap for cleaning.

- What will you use as a sink for the cleanup? I usually use the biggest pot I have. Normally I fill it about 2/3 full of water and have it heating while the meal is being consumed. Then there's room in the pot to add some cold water to adjust the temperature if needed.
- You will also need a dish wand, cloth, or sponge with which to do the washing.
- A heavy-duty scrubber of some kind might be needed for the cleaning of the skillet unless it is a non-stick pan or a cast iron skillet. (A few tablespoons of coarse salt can be useful in scrubbing away anything adhered to the bottom of an iron skillet.)

As you can see from this tiresome example there is an immense number of things to contemplate when planning what to have at hand for meal preparation and later for cleanup. I hope you can also see how picturing each step can help you to think not only of items you may need but also might aid in considering alternative methods for accomplishing a cooking task.

Other Equipment to Consider Bringing

A plastic sheet or small tarp can help to keep your firewood dry.

In order to keep twigs, dirt, or sand from being tracked into your tent you might include a small mat to use as a doormat. We have used one of those split bamboo mats that are sold in beach shops.

Even a doormat might not keep all of the debris from entering the tent, which is a good reason to have a small whisk broom and possibly a dustpan or something such as a sheet of cardboard that could serve as a dustpan.

If feasible in terms of packing space, there may be times when a large, concierge-size umbrella can be a lifesaver. I have cooked more than a few campfire meals under the protection of an umbrella.

Long-handled tongs of the kind that are sold with barbecuing equipment are wonderfully useful when cooking at a campfire.

Pot holders are helpful no matter what cooking method you use and can also be used as hot mats.

A large sponge may be handy to keep at hand just in case your tent leaks.

A sturdy umbrella can be extremely useful during foul weather. Not only can an umbrella aid in keeping you dry but it might also be held over your cooking area during a brief rain shower to keep the rain from putting out your fire.

Extremely large, tough yard waste or contractor trash bags can be extremely handy in more ways than you might imagine. (See particulars in the section on TRASH.)

What to Carry It In

One important rule to bear in mind when packing for a camping trip is that you should try to pack so that the things you will need first are readily accessible. For instance, you won't want to have to dig for the tent (if you are tent camping) because that is the first thing you will want to deal with. If you'll need to eat a sandwich or two before you begin to set up camp, then you'll want the food where you can get to it without too much problem.

When car camping, space is often at a premium - especially in a sedan. If nearly everything must be put in the trunk in order to leave room for passengers then it can be very difficult to tuck equipment and supplies in there with any semblance of order. Often there will be a need to fit items into whatever nook presents itself. Still, every attempt should be made to save the first-needed items to be packed last.

Plastic tubs can help the packing problem immensely when more spacious vehicles are being used. In my opinion it is great to know that the biggest tub is the one that holds the sleeping bags and mattresses while the smaller, green one holds all of the kitchen and food prep items. Having camping stuff stored in tubs is also helpful in terms of storing them after camping season is over (if it ever really is.) The next time your camping gear is needed you can feel somewhat assured that everything is where it was the last time you needed it. It doesn't hurt to inventory all of your goods each time just to be sure nothing important is missing. (Did Sally take one of the sleeping bags to a sleepover at Meagan's? Did we ever get around to buying a replacement for that tent stake that broke?)

I forget whose law it is that states that a thing will expand to encompass all of the space it is allotted. It is certainly true with camping gear. I can recall many camping trips in which every bit of gear fit nicely in the trunk of the car. I later had an old Toyota station wagon that barely held it all. When I bought a pickup there soon was even more camping stuff!

When canoe camping, I made use of a couple of waterproof backpacks for things like clothing and sleeping bags. Unrefrigerated foods were kept in plastic, 5-gallon buckets with lids that sealed tightly. You might acquire some buckets like those for free. The fillings used at donut shops often come in such buckets. The first ones I ever used formerly held pickles that were used by a restaurant. The bucket handles make for easy carrying and can be tied to your canoe without the need for any modifications. In most cases the tightly lidded buckets will even float, should the canoe happen to tip. I have also found rectangular, lidded buckets such as package some brands of kitty litter can be used to protect fragile items. I use a kitty litter bucket of that sort to hold my glass-globed, liquid-fueled lantern.

As I have said before, every camping trip is somehow different. That a certain item was not needed during one particular camping adventure is no assurance that it would not be needed in another. Knowing that makes it very difficult to pare down the quantity of stuff you bring. Still, it is useful and often necessary to take a good look at your gear and decide upon just how essential some of it is.

Just because you can bring something doesn't necessarily mean you must.

Backpackers are extremely aware of the necessity for the evaluation process and most will examine each item to assess its camping value versus its weight. After all, backpackers must carry every single ounce of equipment with them wherever they go. Car campers and even RVers should do the same sifting process, albeit for slightly different reasons.

Limiting the amount of stuff we take with us when camping can sometimes enable us to realize that some items, even items we use in daily life, are of very little importance.

CAMPFIRE SONGS

Among some of the best memories of camping is that of singing songs around the campfire. For some people the singing is their favorite part of the whole camping experience (well, maybe in second place to making and eating s'mores!) If you anticipate singing a few songs it might be helpful to do a little preparation. You might consider bringing along a guitar, ukulele, or some other musical instrument to play along with the singing. Also, it could be a good idea to make yourself a list of songs that might suit the occasion.

In making the list shown here in no particular order of favorites, I consulted a number of lists of best-known campfire songs. Certainly, there are others that could be added. I've included hints to help with remembering some of the more commonly used lyrics.

TOM DOOLEY (Hang down your head/Met her on a mountain/This time tomorrow)

TAVERN IN THE TOWN (And there my true love sits him [her] down./Fare the well for I must leave thee.)

BLOWING IN THE WIND (How many roads must a man walk down/ years-mountain/man-look/people-exist)

DO LORD, OH DO LORD (I've got a home in gloryland/I took Jesus as my Savior)

IF I HAD A HAMMER (song, bell)

KUM-BA-YAH (Someone's singing, praying, laughing, sleeping)

MICHAEL, ROW THE BOAT ASHORE (Sister, help to trim the sail./ River is deep and wide./River Jordan is chilly and cold.)

B-I-N-G-O (There was a farmer who had a dog ...)

GOODNIGHT IRENE (Last Saturday night I got married./Sometimes I live in the country./Stop your rambling; stop your gambling)

WIM-O-WE, THE LION SLEEPS TONIGHT (In the jungle/Near the village/Hush my darling)

ON TOP OF SPAGHETTI (all covered with cheese/It rolled off the table)

PUFF THE MAGIC DRAGON (Together they would travel/A dragon lives forever/His head was bent in sorrow)

FROGGY WENT A COURTIN' (He walked up to Missy Mouse's door/ He said, "Missy Mouse won't you marry me?"/ "Not without my Uncle Rat's consent."/There's bread and cheese upon the shelf.)

ROW, ROW, ROW YOUR BOAT [Can be sung as a round]

RISE UP, O FLAME [Can be sung as a round] (... by thy light glowing. Show to us beauty. Visions endure.)

WHITE CORAL BELLS [Can be sung as a round] (upon a slender stalk. Lily of the Valley bless my garden wall. Oh don't you wish that you could hear them ring? That will happen only when the faeries sing)

SLOOP JOHN B. (We came on .../Hoist up .../The first mate ...)

JAMAICA FAREWELL (Down the way .../But I'm sad to say/Sounds of laughter/Down at the market)

TAKE ME HOME, COUNTRY ROADS (Almost heaven/All my memories/I hear her voice)

AMEN (See the little baby/See Him at the temple/... at the Jordan/ seaside/Marching to Jerusalem/See Him in the garden/Led before Pilate)

WHERE HAVE ALL THE FLOWERS GONE? (young girls/young men/ soldiers/graveyards)

500 MILES (If you miss the train I'm on/Lord I'm one/Not a shirt)

THERE'S A HOLE IN THE BOTTOM OF THE SEA (log/bump/frog/ tail/flea/speck)

WILL THE CIRCLE BE UNBROKEN? (I was standing by the window/ Undertaker/ followed close/went back home)

I'LL FLY AWAY (Some bright morning/When the shadows/Oh, how glad and happy/Just a few more weary days)

RED RIVER VALLEY (From this valley/Come and sit by my side)

I'VE BEEN WORKING ON THE RAILROAD (Can't you hear the whistle blowing/Dinah won't you blow/Someone's in the kitchen)

SWING LOW, SWEET CHARIOT (I looked over Jordan/If you get there before I do)

DOWN IN THE VALLEY (the valley so low/Writing this letter containing three lines/Build me a castle/Roses love sunshine)

AMAZING GRACE ('Twas Grace/Through many dangers/How sweet the name/Must Jesus bear/When we've been here ten thousand years)

HOME, HOME ON THE RANGE (Oh, give me a home ...)

HE'S GOT THE WHOLE WORLD IN HIS HANDS (you and me brother/... sister/... itty bitty baby)

I'M GOING TO LEAVE OLD TEXAS NOW [as a call and response] (... plowed and fenced/I'll say *adiós* to the Alamo/)

THE ERIE CANAL (I had a mule; her name was Sal … /Low bridge. Everybody down.)

WAY DOWN UPON THE SWANEE RIVER (far, far away …/All the world is sad and dreary)

ROCK MY SOUL IN THE BOSOM OF ABRAHAM (So high, low, under, around)

WALTZING MATILDA (Once a jolly swagman sat by the billabong/ Down came a jumbuck/Down came the stockman/Up jumped the swagman)

O SUSANNA (I come from Alabama …/It rained all night the day I left)

SIMPLE GIFTS
'Tis the gift to be simple, 'tis the gift to be free
'Tis the gift to come down where we ought to be,
And when we find ourselves in the place just right,
'Twill be in the valley of love and delight.
When true simplicity is gained,
To bow and to bend we shan't be ashamed,
To turn, turn will be our delight,
Till by turning, turning we come 'round right.

ZIP-A-DEE-DOO-DAH (My oh, my what a beautiful day .../Mr. Bluebird's on my shoulder …)

YOU ARE MY SUNSHINE (The other night, dear, as I lay sleeping)

THE ITSY-BITSY SPIDER (went up the waterspout ...)

COCKLES AND MUSSELS (In Dublin's fair city …/Alive, alive-o …/ She wheeled her wheelbarrow …/Alive, alive-o …)

THIS OLD MAN (nick, knack, paddy-whack song)

KOOKABURRA [Can be sung as a round] (sits in the old gum tree ...)

DO YOUR EARS HANG LOW?
Do your ears hang low?
Do they wobble to and fro?
Can you tie them in a knot?
Can you tie them in a bow?
Can you throw them o'er your shoulder
Like a Continental Soldier?
Do your ears hang low?

THIS LAND IS YOUR LAND (As I went walking/I roamed and rambled)

AS I WENT DOWN IN TO THE RIVER TO PRAY (Oh, sisters, brothers, fathers, mothers, sinners)

OVER THE RAINBOW (Somewhere .../Someday I'll wish ...where troubles melt/... bluebirds fly)

SHE'LL BE COMMING ROUND THE MOUNTAIN (... driving six white horses Whoa back!/... all go out to meet her Hi, babe!/... wearing red pajamas Scratch, scratch - Be sure to do the appropriate hand motions!)

DIXIE (Way down south in the land of cotton/Oh, I wish I was in Dixie)

THERE WAS AND OLD LADY WHO SWALLOWED A FLY (spider, bird, cat, dog, goat, cow, horse)

SIXTEEN TONS (Some people say a man/If you see me coming/I was born one morning when the sun didn't shine/...it was drizzling rain)

HOUSE OF THE RISING SUN (There is a house/mother was a tailor/...only thing a gambler needs/mother, tell your children/...one foot on the platform)

STREETS OF LAREDO (As I walked out/Beat the drum slowly/I can see by your outfit/Go fetch me a cup)

STEWBALL (Stewball was a racehorse/His bridle was silver/fairgrounds were crowded/And way up yonder/I bet on the gray mare/The hoot owl she hollers)

THE WHEELS ON THE BUS (driver-move on back, horn-beep, babies-wah, mommas-shush, wipers-swish)

(UP) OVER MY HEAD (I hear music/light from heaven shining)

WHEN THE SAINTS GO MARCHING IN (sun refuse to shine/moon turns red with blood/trumpet sounds the call)

COTTON FIELDS (When I was a little bitty baby/Now when those cotton fields get rotten/It was down in Louisiana)

GUANTANAMERA (*Yo soy un hombre sincero/ Mi verso es de un verde claro/Por los pobres de la tierra)*

THE BEAR WENT OVER THE MOUNTAIN
The bear went over the mountain,
The bear went over the mountain,
The bear went over the mountain,
To see what he could see.
And all that he could see,
And all that he could see,
Was the other side of the mountain,
The other side of the mountain,
The other side of the mountain,
Was all that he could see.

HAVAH NAGILAH (*Hava neranena/Uru, uru achim*)

ALL THE PRETTY LITTLE HORSES (Hushabye/Dapples and grays, pintos and bays/Way down yonder in the meadow)

POLLY WOLLY DOODLE (Oh, I went down south/Fare the well/My Sal she is a maiden fair-curly eyes and laughing hair)

SHENANDOAH/ACROSS THE WIDE MISSOURI (I long to see you/I'm bound to leave you/I love your daughter)

DOWN BY THE RIVERSIDE (Gonna lay down my sword and shield/ Ain't gonna study war no more/...put on my long, white robe, starry crown, golden shoes)

BUTTERMILK HILL/SHULE AROON (Here I sit on Buttermilk Hill/I'll sell my rock/Oh, my baby, oh my love)

SAKURA [CHERRY BLOOMS] (… noyama mo sato mo/... yayoi no sora wa)

OLD MACDONALD HAD A FARM (And on that farm he had some ducks, cows, chickens, dogs, turkeys, etc.)

CALIFORNIA DREAMIN' (All the leaves are brown/Stopped into a church/...been for a walk on a winter's day)

THE IRISH BALLAD [Rickety-Tickety-Tin] (About a maid I'll sing a song/One morning in a fit of pique/Her mother she could never stand/set her sister's hair on fire/weighted her brother down with stones/One day when she had nothing to do/When at last the police came by/My tragic tale I won't prolong)

MOMMA DON'T ALLOW (no music playing around here/guitar playing/folksong singing/foot stomping/hand clapping)

THE MUFFIN MAN (Oh, do you know …/Yes, I know/Most of us know/All of us know)

FOUND A PEANUT (Cracked it open/It was rotten/Ate it anyway/ Got a stomach ache/Called the doctor/Penicillin/ Operation/I died anyway/Went to heaven/ Wouldn't take me/Went the other way/ Wouldn't take me/Then I woke up/Found a peanut)

THIS LITTLE LIGHT OF MINE (All around my neighborhood/Every single place I go/When my friend is feeling low)

GETTING READY TO CAMP

If you already own a tent you should, if at all possible, pitch it in a sunny spot in your yard for a day or two, a week or so before your first trip of the season. If you already have a tent and it hasn't been used for a long time, set it up and use a garden hose to wash your tent's inside and then the outside. Wipe the inside walls and then the floor with a small, terry washcloth or similar hand towel soaked with water or in a solution of 1part white vinegar to 4 parts water if needed to remove musty smells and/or to aid in removing any mold. Then hose and wipe the outside. No soap or scrubbing should ever be used as to do so may damage any protective coating the tent fabric may have. A scrub brush might also leave fibers stuck in the zippers which could cause serious problems later.

As you hose your tent be sure to carefully spray the zippers to remove any grit or other material that could impair proper function. Allow the sun to dry the tent thoroughly, then apply seam sealer to all seams and silicone lubricant/waterproofing to the zippers. You will find numerous seam sealers and zipper lubricants at your local outfitters or online. Ignore any advice you may receive that discusses the use of petroleum jelly on the zippers. Gooey stuff like that allows dirt and grit to become attached to the zippers and could cause malfunctions. (See the section on WEATHER for more about seam sealers.)

Here is a cautionary tale: A friend once performed most of these cleaning tasks on his tent. The bright sun was quickly drying the tent as my friend eagerly anticipated using his clean-smelling tent on an upcoming family outing. He never imagined that his male cat might feel a need to mark the tent as his territory!

Any sleeping bags you plan to use should be removed from their protective sacks and fluffed. Fluffing can be done by hand or by running one bag at a time in the dryer on a "air fluff," "air dry" or "no heat" setting. For best results toss in a couple of "dryer balls" or tennis balls. If possible, the bags should be opened completely and hung in the sun for a couple hours, turning them over at least once.

If space permits, a day or so prior to your trip, your camping equipment should be laid out where you can inventory it to be sure all you need is there. A checklist could certainly be helpful to ensure that you have it all. This is the time in which you might remember having loaned your camp stove or air mattress to someone who forgot to return it. You might discover that you somehow left behind one of your tent poles when you broke camp last time. Better to discover that now instead of when you arrive at the campground.

SETTING UP CAMP

Once you have arrived at your chosen campsite there are some things to do before you begin setting up camp. First, take a good look at how the campsite is laid out. If there is a picnic table and if it isn't anchored in place, is it where it will best suit your needs? Is there enough space between the table and the campfire to be safe? Is the table close enough to the fire to be handy if you plan to cook on the fire? Do you need to relocate the table to allow more room for your tent or RV?

If you will be tent camping it is extremely important to survey the area where the tent will be to ensure the ground is free of sticks, rocks or nuts. Such things can not only tear holes in the floor of your tent but also can make for very uncomfortable sleeping.

Almost without exception, pitching the tent, if you are using one, should be the first item of business. Often you will find that you need lots of room around the tent in order to manipulate the poles that constitute the framework of your tent. You will also need a bit of ground around the tent to accommodate the staking of it and some space allowed for guy ropes and tiedowns.

Sometimes space for guy ropes is somewhat limited. One solution is to make use of a "crutch." I call it a crutch only because it somewhat resembles one. Locate or create a forked stick of a length equal to the height of the line of pull needed. Place the crutch with the shaft of it more or less upright a short distance from the guy rope's point of origin. Run the guy rope over the fork and then angle the rope downward to where it can be staked. The use of the crutch will effectively shorten the length of the guy rope while still maintaining the desired angle of pull. I have sometimes found myself camping in areas where such a stick was difficult to find. At a hardware store I stumbled upon a solution. There is a commercially made pole that is designed to support a sagging clothesline. Two of them are now kept with my tent camping equipment.

CAMPFIRE

Many people would agree that there is something very special about a campfire. A campfire lends an atmosphere to camping as few other things can. At night it supplies a soul-warming, flickering glow that can almost magically conjure long-forgotten memories, wistfulness, and reverie. A late-night campfire seems to engender quiet voices and tales of days gone by or perhaps even a ghost story or two. A campfire might also serve as a source of warmth or as a means for cooking.

Much of what I have to say on this subject is directed toward those who would enjoy cooking over an open fire. It may, though, be your intent to have a campfire purely for atmosphere. You want to watch the light from the flames dance in playful silhouettes on the tent walls and sparkle in the eyes of the faces gathered round the fire and to smell the delicious smoke. You may also envisage campfires from bygone years, take joy from hearing the wood pop and squeal. After all, there are few experiences equal to watching the sparks that seem to fly up to become one with the stars and to feeling at last that you are truly camping!

I greatly appreciate all aspects of creating and enjoying a campfire. However, even if you are well versed in making a campfire, sometimes it can be a daunting challenge, despite what you may have seen in the movies.

I don't recommend the use of fires consisting of bagged charcoal or made through the use of petroleum-based, quid flammables. Charcoal as we usually see it today is often little more than powdered coal combined with some partially burned wood fibers that has been compressed into small blocks. Unless you have been living on another planet for the past few years you already know that when coal is burned it releases countless toxins.

Virtually all of the liquid flammables often used to start charcoal fires are petroleum-based and release toxins of their own when burned. Because charcoal and most liquid flammables can release noxious fumes, I find the concept of inhaling those fumes or of putting food in contact with either or both as something to be scrupulously avoided. Besides this I have seen far too many people misuse the liquids in very dangerous ways, including squirting the liquids onto open flames, risking a backfire and horrible injury. (See the section on Fire Safety.)

Firewood

There are countless books that explain various methods of fire starting. Some will have you shredding cedar bark or saving dryer lint and/or striking flints with pocket knives. Nearly all of that is great information if you are attempting to survive in the woods; but I'm going to tell you what you might need for starting a fire at a campground or perhaps in a few other settings.

Probably the single most overlooked fire making basic is that you must start small. The reality is that it would be difficult to find materials too small for the purpose. One savvy woodsman advised, "Start at the top of the tree and work downward." By that he meant that you should begin with the tiniest of twigs at the ends of branches and gradually add larger and larger twigs and eventually work up to thicker branches and wood from the trunks of trees.

Small wood or kindling is sometimes unavailable or extremely difficult to find because previous campers may have already picked up most of it. This is highly likely to be the case when you camp later in the season at an organized campground. You may need to create your own kindling from larger pieces. This operation is most safely done while wearing heavy gloves to protect your hands from possible injury. If you don't know how to split wood then it is best to not attempt it until you have watched someone else who does.

Places that sell kiln-dried firewood might also sell bundles of kindling. Some of them even offer free kindling. It won't hurt to ask. An alternative might be to bring a few "surveyors' stakes" or even a bundle of wooden shims that can be purchased relatively cheaply at a hardware or home improvement store.

A song about moonshiners says, "Don't use no green or rotten wood. They'll catch you by the smoke." Dry, seasoned wood produces minimal smoke. Most campgrounds prohibit the use of green wood such as you might get by cutting down trees that are still alive. "Dead and down" are usually the key words campgrounds will use when depicting what wood they authorize you to collect within the campground.

Please note the "and" in the phrase, "dead and down." In nearly all instances both conditions must be present. To avoid unnecessary smoke don't use branches that may have fallen due to high winds and that still have green leaves attached. (Besides, they are extremely resistant to breaking into usable lengths.) Likewise, don't use soft, crumbly rotten wood. Rotten wood can soak up water like a sponge. Besides being difficult to ignite, rotten wood, as the song says, will produce immense amounts of smoke - often quite acrid and foul-smelling smoke.

Care and alertness should be used when searching for "dead and down" wood or kindling. This is particularly true where poisonous snakes might be in the vicinity. Make it a habit to look carefully around the location of a likely looking stick before you reach for it. Snakebites, even those of nonpoisonous snakes are not fun. At minimum a snakebite is likely to precipitate the need for a tetanus shot.

Another thing to watch for is poison ivy or poison oak. Learn to recognize them – especially poison ivy in all of its forms. Downed wood that has reddish, hairy vines on it is something to avoid. Consider the possibilities when you send your kids into the woods to look for kindling. (See the section on Plants under GENERAL SAFETY.)

Hardwoods burn longer and cleaner than soft woods. Kiln-dried wood sold in camp stores and even in grocery stores is always hardwood. Hardwood is the best wood to use for most purposes and is the only kind to use for campfire cooking. Pinewood is considered to be a soft wood. If you happen upon some dead and down pine you will find it burns readily and therefore is great for starting a fire. It burns very quickly and produces a lot of heat. However, pinewood should always be avoided when cooking at a campfire. Pine emits lots of soot as it burns which can irrevocably impart disagreeable flavors to anything it contacts.

Recent awareness of certain infestations by various harmful insects and fungi have brought about numerous restrictions regarding firewood. Forested areas have become at risk due to problems with, for example, Emerald Ash Borer beetles, Gypsy Moth larvae, and a particular fungus that quickly kills white pine trees. In many campgrounds and most especially in many state and federal campgrounds it is prohibited to bring firewood that is not locally harvested, kiln-dried, or otherwise specifically approved. Be a good steward of our forests by not bringing in firewood you know to be unauthorized.

Cutting and Splitting Firewood

As romantic as the image of a burly woodsman chopping at a log might be, it doesn't take long when actually doing it to know what hard work it truly is. The difficulty could never be more apparent than when someone attempts the task with a dull hatchet. There are other means of accomplishing this chore.

If you should happen upon a large but portable branch or small tree that is "dead and down" you will want to make it into lengths to fit your fire ring. In fact, most campgrounds prohibit the use of wood that projects beyond the fire ring. One rather handy alternative to chopping is to make use of leverage. Find a couple of large trees that are quite close together or make use of a fork in the trunk of a single tree. Push the desired length of your candidate for firewood through the opening made by the two trunks, smaller end first. Next, using one tree trunk as a fulcrum, apply as much pressure to the "candidate" as necessary to break off a section. As you work toward the thicker part of your branch or small tree the task will become more difficult. Where feasible I do the pushing with my hips. If you can't break the wood by this method then you are left with three other options.

- You can chop the remainder into smaller pieces.
- You can saw it into chunks that are more useful.
- You can search for a better candidate.

Hatchets are simply not designed for the purpose of cutting through thick wood. The handle of a hatchet is too short to allow any real power to be put into a swing. Where hatchets shine is in the task of splitting wood for kindling. Axes, on the other hand, are well suited for chopping. The handle of an ax is long enough to make best use of the weight of the ax head to convey the power from each swing to the point of the ax head. If space and weight aren't important issues for you then an ax is a good option.

Personally, I like to use what many call a "boy's ax," not to be confused with a "campers' ax" which is just a hatchet with a slightly longer handle. The head of a boy's ax is just a bit smaller than that of a regular ax and the handle is a few inches shorter. Yet the boy's ax is surprisingly powerful as well as versatile for accomplishing most of the tasks of a bigger ax as well as for the smaller jobs of the hatchet. Whatever you choose will be of little use to you unless you learn how to keep it properly sharp. Use a flat file to smooth out nicks and for general sharpening.

Proper technique for chopping wood is first to ensure the piece is well anchored. Make the first cut at a relatively sharp angle then follow with a similar cut from the opposite direction a couple of inches away, thus loosening a small wedge or chip. Repeat this process, leaving an ever-widening, V-shaped notch, until the wood is cut completely through. Prior to the final chops be sure to place a piece of wood under the piece being cut to prevent the ax blade from cutting into the ground, thus possibly dulling the ax head.

Even when an ax is handled properly there can be accidents. Small children should never be allowed to wield an ax. Children old enough to chop wood should already be aware that living trees should never be chopped.

Another option for your large chunk of wood is to saw it. Sawing with a good saw can be an extremely efficient method for cutting wood - and quieter, by the way. There are some great saws available for the job as well as some that are complete wastes of time and energy.

Before discussing saws more it is probably worth pointing out that most campgrounds strictly forbid the use of chainsaws and some even prohibit battery-powered chain saws or saber-saws.

When you look for a hand-powered saw you should avoid any that will not produce a good kerf. A kerf is the thin valley created by the saw-blade as it cuts through the wood and can also refer to the width of the cutting edge of the blade. If the kerf is only as wide as the blade, itself, then the saw will almost invariably become pinched or stuck in the wood it is cutting. The main problem with such a sawblade is that it is incapable of removing the cut material from the valley or notch it has created. A good, wide kerf is produced by a blade that has teeth that are offset (bent outward) enough to protrude beyond the width of the blade. A sawblade with a wide kerf will push out the sawdust it creates and is unlikely to become pinched.

You should also pay attention to the number of points per inch of blade. More points per inch creates a finer, neater cut - something you should care nothing about when cutting firewood. I prefer to use a small, compact crosscut handsaw that sports something close to 9 teeth per inch and is advertised as some sort of super saw or as a distant relative of a shark because of its comparatively broad kerf and the amazing way it seems to bite its way through wood.

As mentioned above, the third and most obvious option for what to do with your oversize piece of wood is to fling it back where it came from and to go find another piece. I am not one to put huge amounts of effort into re-sizing wood. If it won't break then it usually gets discarded. It normally takes much less effort to search out another candidate than to saw or chop it into desired lengths.

Tinder

Tinder is one of the most important components of firemaking. In olden times, a scrap of charred, cotton cloth was kept dry to be used as tinder for the making of a fire by use of a flint. If other dry material could be found, such things as pieces of birch bark, dead and dry plant material, or pine needles might have been used. Dry pine cones burned well also.

Today there are many fire-starting aids commercially available that make firemaking somewhat simpler. This is not to say that the use of tinder is never needed, but sometimes can be bypassed if great care is used. Most fire-starting aids employ fine bits of wood or sawdust combined with a wax or wax-like substance and are formed into small sticks or cubes. Setting alight a corner or edge of a "firestick," as they are sometimes called, usually requires just a single match or brief use of a lighter. Once the firestick is flaming well, you can begin adding the tiniest twigs you can find - often no bigger than matchsticks. As the twigs become engulfed by flame increasingly larger twigs or sticks can be added. Be sure to allow the flames time to catch fire to the previous addition before adding more. In very little time you may add full-size logs.

You can create your own firesticks or fire starters. Place an empty, paper pulp egg carton on a solid, nonporous surface. A cookie sheet could serve. Fill each section of the carton about halfway with sawdust. Then drizzle melted wax over each sawdust-filled chamber, using enough wax to cover the sawdust. Allow to dry and then tear or cut apart each section. Now you have a dozen good fire starters. Note that you can acquire the wax needed among the canning supply section of most grocery stores. Otherwise, you can melt a few old, used candles for the purpose. Please use caution when attempting this project. Hot wax can cause a serious burn injury.

Another homemade fire starter that is easy to make uses a collection of dryer lint. I have been told that you can also soak cotton balls with melted petroleum jelly. I have used the former successfully, but have not yet tried the cotton ball and petroleum jelly trick. I can only imagine making them as being a messy project and unfortunately involves burning a petroleum product.

Even if firesticks or starters are available, tinder of the kinds mentioned above also might also be used in conjunction - especially if your kindling is wet with rain. While some tinder is easier to light than others, its use, or the use of a fire starter, is foundational to getting a fire going. The process, once the tinder is aflame, is exactly as stated above - add tiny twigs and build up to larger and larger ones.

It might be worth remembering that in a pinch, most kinds of the snack-style corn chips burn surprisingly well - certainly for long enough to get your smallest twigs aflame.

Location of Your Fire

In most campgrounds the location of the fire ring is predetermined. Some are either staked to the ground or mounted in concrete. But if you are allowed to choose the location for your fire there are some things you should consider. Wind direction is important. You probably wouldn't want to spend your night in a tent filled with smoke. If you are camped on a hillside, particularly if there is a lake or stream farther down the hill, you should know that the air down the hill will most likely drift uphill as the morning progresses; but will more or less reverse direction in the evening. If possible, it is probably a good idea to place your tent to one side or the other of the direction of airflow as it relates to the likely path of your campfire's smoke.

Site Preparation for Your Campfire

When camping at an organized campground you will usually find the area surrounding the fire ring is completely clear of anything flammable. However, when rough camping this is not often the case. Once you have chosen the location for your fire you should clear an area approximately five feet in diameter from the center of where your fire will be. Tall grass, leaves, twigs, and anything else that might catch on fire should be removed.

Fire Rings, Fire Pits, Etc.

Most campgrounds have what are sometimes euphemistically called fire rings. Some are nothing more than rusty old car or truck wheels that often do not include a grate. Others are somewhat more elaborately fabricated and frequently come with adjustable cast iron grates. When choosing a campsite where such conveniences are available it is important to take a good look at the fire ring to ensure it is fully functional, is relatively level, or will at least suit your needs - especially if you have plans to cook on it. Anyone who has ever attempted to fry eggs in a pan on a slanted grate knows how frustrating it can be to have the cooking oil and eggs to slide to the lower side of the pan.

Grates

If there is an adjustable grate at your campsite check to make sure it can actually be moved up or down. Some you may find are so rusted or bent by extreme heat that adjustment isn't possible. In any case, if you plan to cook on the campfire, it is best to come with a sturdy grate of your own to use if none is provided or if the one provided is somehow inadequate. Often, for instance, the adjustable grate furnished will not allow you to place your food close enough to the coals. Any grate you bring must be sturdy enough to hold your food or your heaviest pot or pan over high heat without caving in or dumping your food into the fire.

One of the most versatile grates is mounted upon an iron stake that you drive into the ground next to the fire. The grate is configured so it can be raised or lowered and can also swing to a position over the fire or away from it. There are also some well-made grates that mount upon tripods and can be raised or lowered as needed by way of small metal chains.

Note that much of the rust you will probably find on fire ring grates will flake off when the grate is placed over a hot fire. However, if you have a grill brush (or you might make use of the end of a thick stick) you can scrape off most of the rust not removed by the fire.

When using a grate to cook foods directly over the heat the process will go better if the grate is lightly oiled before the food is placed upon it. Gee (clarified butter) or coconut oil are the best for withstanding the high temperatures, but most oils will serve the purpose. I usually use a folded paper towel to smear the oil onto the grate. Fireproof tongs can be helpful.

Never, ever use any kind of aerosol near a fire! Cooking oils - especially in the form of aerosol sprays - are very flammable. The use of them near a flame risks the possibility of severe injury. If you must use an aerosol oil spray, first remove the grill from the fire. Alternatively, spray the oil onto a paper towel before coating the grill.

Rocks

If there is no fire ring available where you camp it will more than likely be obvious where others before you have made their campfires and you should follow suit unless there is something unsafe about that location. For instance, there could be a tree branch hanging too low over the previously used spot. When a metal fire ring isn't present most people appreciate having a stone ring of sufficient diameter and height to enclose a fire and to support a grate, if needed. If the rocks you use have any moisture trapped within them, they can and often will explode when exposed to high heat. If you must build a rock ring you should include a large, flat stone close by. It can be very handy as a place to set a pot when you remove it from the fire. A rock ring should only be constructed in "rustic camping" situations.

If a fire ring is provided, use it. Do not attempt to "improve" it by the addition of large rocks. Most campgrounds and all national parks and national forests forbid such actions. The reasons are many. Most state and national parks as well as state and national forests view not only the trees and plants but also all rocks as part of the natural resource that their employees are sworn to protect. They are strong advocates of a "leave it as you found it" attitude and can even impose fines for misuse of natural resources. It is entirely possible that the camper who comes after you may not want to have rocks in the fire ring. I can assure you that campground maintenance workers and camp hosts despise having to remove rocks over and over again after each succession of campers who put rocks in the fire pits.

How to Start and Maintain A Campfire

Making a campfire is not usually difficult if the necessary materials are available along with a clear idea of how they should be used.

I once discovered a novice camper who captured my attention because he had an impressive pile of burnt wooden matches where he knelt in front of his fire ring. The man had become quite frustrated after making numerous unsuccessful attempts to set fire to a section of a log that was at least a foot in diameter and nearly that tall. He had placed the huge chunk of wood onto nothing more than a small bed of dry leaves. The leaves burned readily; but the wood was merely scorched. He soon learned there is much more to building a campfire.

Arrange Your Fuel

Before you begin to make a fire, you should lay out your materials where you can reach them easily in order to feed the fire as it grows. Ideally, you should have three or even four piles of kindling divided by size, beginning with matchstick thickness to pencil-thick. Another pile could contain sticks as thick as your index finger or slightly thicker. The thickness should increase with pieces of wood at least the circumference of your forearm comprising the last pile. Some camping source books advocate having as many of the matchstick and pencil-thick twigs as you can hold in one hand. However, if the kindling is damp or even wet, I prefer to make good use of lots more of the matchstick thick pieces. An armload of finger-thick wood should be next. Then you should have another good-sized pile of larger wood. You will almost invariably need more of the larger wood than you estimate.

I find it helpful to break the thinnest pieces into lengths of less than a foot. I break the rest of the wood into somewhat longer pieces.

Matches and Lighters

You should have a source of flame and something that will burn quite easily to get the fire started. Anyone who has attempted to start a fire on a rainy day by using "book matches" can attest to how useless they can be at times. Wooden safety matches can be nice to have, but are equally useless when the required striking surface gets damp. Stores sell a wide variety of waterproof containers for matches of which very few include striking surfaces that are also waterproof or even at all useful. Many camping books go into great detail about how to preserve and protect wooden matches. If you prefer to use wooden matches then there is a wealth of information to be found as to how to coat them with fingernail polish or some other waterproofing. Or there are some commercially produced, "waterproof" matches; but again, the striking surface must be perfectly dry for any of them to work. "Strike anywhere" matches, such as you may have seen in old cowboy movies, have become increasingly difficult to obtain due to certain shipping restrictions retailers must now observe.

Few things, though, are handier than a good cigarette lighter so long as its flint wheel is kept dry. Zippo lighters are good to have because the flint is normally covered until needed. That style of lighter is relatively windproof as well. If you choose a lighter of that kind then be sure to fill it with fluid before your camping trip. An extra flint can be stored under the felt-like piece that covers the absorbent material inside the lighter. Some other styles of lighters are often quite inexpensive and so it may prove helpful to have a few extras stored in waterproof plastic bags and tucked away in various locations as back-ups. It should be mentioned also that there are some lighters for sale that are reputed to be waterproof. Reviews for waterproof lighters that I have seen are mostly favorable.

Fire Configurations

Although there are very many configurations for creating a fire lay, my favorites are the "log cabin" and "tepee" or a combination of both. The "log cabin" form is especially good when making a large campfire that will last for hours almost without intervention. You build the base of the "cabin" by laying a few of your largest pieces of wood parallel with each other to form something close to a square. It is best to leave just a little space between the pieces for air flow. The next layer is placed crosswise to the first and consists of wood that is somewhat less thick. This pattern of stacking continues, using less and less thick pieces, until just prior to placing the final layer you place your tinder or fire-starter. Once your topmost layer is set ablaze the fire will gradually consume each layer down to the bottom. (I often build a teepee fire at the top.) Because it burns down slowly this fire lay works best as an ornamental fire or one that is not expected to be used for cooking or roasting marshmallows for quite a while.

The "tepee" fire lay is great for dealing with damp firewood because the fire consumes the inner part while drying the outer pieces. It is constructed by leaning progressively thicker pieces of wood against each other forming a conical pile around your tinder or fire-starter, making sure to leave an opening on the windward side so that you can ignite the inner core.

Another good fire lay is the "lean-to" style. For this you would lay down a somewhat large, backstop piece of firewood crosswise to yourself and place your tinder or fire-starter along the near side of it. Light the tinder and quickly begin to lean layers of wood lengthwise in ever increasing thicknesses perpendicularly against the backstop piece. Continue the process until you gradually work up to your largest wood.

One more useful fire lay called a "star fire," is useful when a small, steady fire is wanted. It can begin with a relatively small "tepee" fire at the center of much larger wood that is arranged radially around the "tepee" in a starburst fashion. In this arrangement the larger pieces are pushed toward the center as they are consumed by the fire.

The Shape of Your Fire

For most purposes a campfire area is round. After all, much of the heat from a campfire radiates outward from a central point. In campgrounds the fire rings are, well... rings. Even most of the rustic campfire spots consist of circles of stones, often already in existence. However, any discussion of campfires - particularly those upon which cooking is to be done - should make mention of keyhole fires.

A keyhole fire is an arrangement in which there is a main, usually circular, body of fire as well as a relatively narrow strip of burning coals that have been raked from the main fire. The overall shape of this fire is named for the old-fashioned keyholes that consisted of a round portion that had an intersecting, essentially oblong part at its base. The purpose of the keyhole fire is to have a bed of coals over which to stretch a grate to cook upon. Dependent upon the size of a skillet or pot and the width of the oblong area, a grill might not be necessary. More coals can be added from the main fire as they are needed.

I find the keyhole fire arrangement especially useful when broiling steaks or burgers in a campground fire ring. Although I cannot reconfigure the ring, itself, I can scrape a few coals from the main fire to one area and can thereby place my own grate closer to the coals than the fire ring's construction might normally allow. In rustic areas I can usually arrange stones into a much more serviceable, keyhole configuration. (Please also see the Cooking Over A Fire section of CAMPFIRE COOKING.)

Mistakes When Firemaking

The most common error in starting a campfire is that of adding too much wood, or wood that is too large, too soon. Take time to make sure each addition has fully ignited before adding more. Remember that oxygen is equally as important to fire as heat and fuel. Make sure your fire has "room to breathe."

I usually pride myself in my ability to start a fire with a single match or else a single use of a cigarette lighter. Sometimes, though, the "fire gods" are not working with me and the fire refuses to burst into flame, despite my efforts. Over time I have learned that it is far better to admit defeat after a few minutes of desperately blowing or fanning a fire. There comes a time when I must dismantle my fire lay in order to start over rather than to make repeated attempts to restart the fire as it stands.

If anyone happens to be monitoring my activities I will, in my most authoritative voice, state that the wood was somehow just too damp. If the area has been perfectly arid for weeks, I may have no choice but to admit to having added too much wood too quickly and then "expertly" reconstruct my fire lay, taking care to be a bit slower and more patient with any additions of fuel. Most of the time I can start the reincarnation of the fire with one match...er...lighter.

The Rule of Threes

After all cooking is done and/or if the fire needs only to be perpetuated ornamentally or for warmth, I add logs in threes. Keeping the logs horizontal and more or less parallel with each other, I place one on either side of the existing coals or burning wood. I place the third one, usually the largest, on top of the two. In this way the heat produced by the burning of the smaller two logs will roast the larger one. It makes for a warm and visually pleasing campfire. One reason I prefer this style of fire is that I find a tepee fire a little troublesome when it comes to adding more logs as well as that the wood seems to burn too quickly.

Campfires and Trash

When camping in wilderness or other remote areas you will need to remember that any trash or garbage you create will need to leave with you when you depart. Camping in such locations and in reality, anywhere else, should always be of minimal impact to the environment. "Pack it in; pack it out." "Take nothing but pictures; leave nothing but footprints." You have probably seen these slogans before. What they mean with regard to trash is that none should be buried or otherwise be left behind.

During a particularly lengthy stay in an isolated camping area you may find it necessary to burn the food residue out of cans to help reduce unpleasant smells or enticements for scavengers; but the burnt cans should be removed from the campfire and once they have cooled, should be put into a trash bag or other suitable container for you to transport for appropriate disposal.

Virtually all campgrounds have dumpsters available in which to deposit your trash. Some even have containers for recycling such things as aluminum cans, glass bottles, and plastics. Read the posted instructions carefully because not all places are able to process certain recyclables.

One thing you should never do at a campground is to burn your trash in your fire ring or pit. Just because something seems to be flammable does not necessarily mean that it should be burned. In the first place, there are some things that simply will not burn. They may melt; but they will not burn or won't burn completely at the temperatures of most campfires. Among these items are aluminum cans and glass bottles. If the fire is hot enough the glass or aluminum may become melted blobs, but they will remain blobs long after the fire is gone. Glass may shatter long before it gets hot enough to melt. Some things require extremely high heat or repeated burnings to become significantly diminished. Bones, steel cans and eggshells are among this group.

There are also some things that should never, ever be burned. Plastics of nearly any kind and Styrofoam release harmful, gaseous residues when burned. If you have ever smelled them burning then you now know the stench should be thought of as a warning that it is a bad idea to burn these. In addition, the smell of burning trash and garbage can spread far beyond your own campsite to offend the nostrils of your fellow campers and to pollute the surrounding air.

All too often in my role as a camp host or even as a camper I have had to clean out the nasty leavings of someone who attempted to burn trash in the fire circle or fire ring. I have pulled some amazing things from the ashes. Not only have there been broken bottles, scorched aluminum cans, corn cobs and chicken bones, but I once discovered the remains of a BB rifle, including its melted plastic stock. I had to wonder at what sort of story lay behind that. I have also seen where someone placed empty plastic water bottles upon the grate, presumably just to watch them partially burn and then to become one with the grate. I think the most astonishing thing about folks who burn such items in the fire pits is their seemingly oblivious disregard for any camper who comes afterward to use that fire pit.

Put Your Fire Out

The most important thing to know about a campfire is how to put it out - DEAD OUT. The way to put out any fire is to remove any or all of its components, fuel, oxygen, and heat. By dispersing the fuel so that the burning pieces aren't in close proximity to each other, you can partially remove the fuel of the fire. The heat (as well as some oxygen) can be removed by liberally sprinkling the coals, ashes, and actively burning pieces with increasing amounts of water. Use a stick to stir and invert these until no more smoke arises. Then stir the ashes again and check to see that nothing was missed. Dig down a bit. You will be surprised at how much heat is retained beneath the former fire. Repeat the process as many times as is needed to ensure that the heat of the fire has been extinguished. Note that it is wise to stand upwind and at arm's length when applying the water in order to avoid exposure to steam and/or flying ashes. If in doubt as to wind direction, sprinkle the ashes with a very small amount of water to check.

Fire Safety

Far too many burns involving charcoal grills are caused by misuse of lighter fluid or gasoline. Usually the misuse occurs when impatience compels someone to attempt to augment a charcoal grill fire that has already been ignited. Logically, it would also be a bad idea to do the same with a campfire. Why would you risk injury and the spoiling of a camping trip by trying to boost a fire in that way?

A campfire is a great place for teaching a child fire safety. The tangible heat of a campfire is a far cry from what they might feel at home through a forced air heating system. One thing a child should be taught even before the campfire is lit is that there is to be no running or horseplay anywhere near the fire. Often it is helpful to specify wide boundaries within which such behavior will not be tolerated. The reason for this rule should be clearly explained. It only takes a small stumble or loss of footing to bring about some very serious burns.

If it is much too windy to get your fire going, it should be taken as a warning that starting it is probably not a good idea. A strong wind can carry live cinders and ashes quite far. Depending upon the direction of the wind, your tent could suffer damage. Your tent should be a minimum of fifteen feet from the fire if at all possible.

Never start a fire until you have at hand the means for putting it out. If your fire should happen to get out of control somehow you won't want to choose that moment to have to fetch the means for extinguishing it. Water works best for wood fires because it removes heat and some oxygen at the same time. Dirt or sand are in second place as fire suppressants because they are only capable of removing oxygen. Whichever you may have readily available, gather a sufficient quantity and have it ready before you start your fire. Also, as mentioned before, be sure to have cleared an area within an approximately five-foot radius of your fire.

Never, ever leave a fire unattended. Unless you have eyes on your fire, it is unattended. If you are camping alone you should plan ahead and make any trips to the bathroom before you start your fire. If you are inside your tent you probably cannot see your fire, particularly if you are napping. If you should need to leave your campsite momentarily then some other member of your party should be put in charge of the fire. If that isn't possible then ask a fellow camper to keep an eye on your fire during your brief absence. Remember, though, that responsibility for that fire ultimately rests with you.

Marshmallows

Roasting marshmallows is probably the most favorite of all campfire activities. It can also be quite dangerous. Kids (and some adults) are generally not accustomed to thinking about the potential consequences of waiving around a long, pointed stick with or without a hot or even flaming marshmallow on the end of it. Your job is to make sure each camper is given a slot near enough to the fire to do the roasting but far enough from others to minimize the possibility of burns or even impalement. If the area around the fire becomes too crowded then turns must be taken.

My own preference is for my marshmallows to be toasted to a golden brown; others prefer theirs to be burnt. In either case a hot marshmallow can become quite gooey and will readily adhere to almost anything it touches – including skin. To prevent possible contact burns, hot marshmallows should never be held near or above exposed skin. If a marshmallow is to be eaten from the stick safely, a roasted marshmallow should be held below chest level and far away from anyone who could accidentally jostle the one holding the stick. If you believe your child is too young, too small, or too active to safely participate in this activity alone then you should volunteer to roast their marshmallows or else to do some hands-on assisting.

GENERAL SAFETY

Camping adventures have the potential to bring you into unfamiliar areas or situations. You may find that there can be far more opportunities for the dangers of poisoning. There are countless areas that can contain creatures or even plants with the capability of delivering poisons. Best known of these are poisonous snakes, but there are also scorpions, certain spiders, wasps, hornets, and bees. Perhaps the most important thing to know about any of these animals is that for the most part they will not go out of their way to bite or sting. Doing so is most often their only recourse as a defensive measure to a perceived threat. There are other kinds of poisons in the wild. Some plants are extremely poisonous if consumed. Other plants have the capability of producing unparalleled itching or discomfort that requires a mere touch by bare skin to induce.

Snakebites

It is extremely important to know what kinds of poisonous or venomous snakes you might encounter and what to do if that encounter results in a bite. Preparation is sometimes vital. If you are camping in an area where poisonous snakes are common then having access to appropriate treatment and antivenins could quite suddenly become extremely important. Be sure you know who to contact when you or someone you witness has been bitten. It is important for the one who is bitten to try to remain calm. A slower heart rate can also slow the spread of the poison. Please note that cutting of any kind is no longer part of any recommended treatment of snakebites. What is recommended is the soonest possible treatment by someone medically trained for the purpose. (Please see the section on Snakes in the WILDLIFE section for more information.)

Scorpion Stings

Although in the United States stings from scorpions do not normally result in deaths, scorpion stings can be extremely uncomfortable, sometimes compared to wasp stings, and can result in some very undesirable after-effects.

My father grew up in Texas. It was his habit as a boy to leave his shoes and his only pair of jeans in a pile at the foot of his bed at night. One morning, after donning a fresh shirt, he pulled on his jeans and was about to lace up his shoes when he was stung by a scorpion. It was somewhere in his jeans. Dad was stung nearly a dozen times before he could pull off his jeans. You can be sure that he always checked both his jeans and his shoes from then on!

Black Widow and Brown Recluse Spider Bites

Both black widow and brown recluse spiders prefer out-of-the-way areas where they are not likely to be disturbed. If you happen to see one crawling around it is more than likely trying to find such an area. These two are the only truly poisonous spiders in the continental United States. Although their bites can result in the need for medical intervention, infants are among the very few at risk of death from either spider's bite.

Most people know that in the U.S. the bulbous, shiny, black body of a black widow has a bright red hourglass-shaped marking on its underside that may also include a small red dot. The markings are somewhat different in other parts of the world.

While the black widow gets most of the attention, I should mention that there is also a brown widow that shares many similarities except for coloration. The brown widow's slightly smaller, rounded body often looks more like polished wood and the hourglass is more toward orange or yellow in color. It also has striped legs. But you are unlikely to encounter this spider in the USA unless you are in Hawaii or in Southern California.

The brown recluse spider is sometimes also known as a "fiddleback" because of the violin-shaped marking seen on its back. The brown recluse is also known to seek out areas where they are not likely to be intruded upon.

Most spiders are not aggressive, but will attack if disturbed. Widow spiders and brown recluse spiders both share that characteristic. More often than not, the people who are bitten by spiders of any kind have, perhaps quite innocently, put their hands into a secluded place that has been more or less abandoned for a time.

A tarantula native to the U.S. can deliver a bite that some people might equate with the pain of a bee sting, but the bites are nowhere nearly as poisonous as the black widow and brown recluse. It should be pointed out, though, that although tarantula bites can be quite unpleasant, death is very rarely the end result.

Wasp, Hornet, and Bee Stings

There are countless varieties of wasps and hornets, and bees. Some of each are relatively docile while others are extremely aggressive and easily agitated. Most people are acquainted with these creatures.

While mud daubers, the wasps that create those clay-like groupings of tubes in the eves of houses and other sheltered places, are generally non-aggressive, most wasps will readily defend their nests. Hornets, are virtually all quite aggressive when defending their nesting sites. Bees, with the exception of certain non-native species, are comparatively non-aggressive.

Nearly anyone who has attempted to have a picnic where others have done the same, has discovered yellow-jackets. Yellow-jackets are normally less than half an inch long and have alternating stripes of yellow and black that encircle much of their bodies. They are particularly attracted to picnic grounds where fruits or sugary drinks may be common. Usually, while they are on a food-finding mission they won't display aggression. However, when someone gets too close to one of their nests, they become extremely defensive and/or aggressive.

Most people who have spent much time outdoors have accidentally met with wasps, hornets and bees. Just about all of these folks have stories to share about when, where, and how they were stung or how they narrowly escaped being stung. Virtually all would have to admit that the creatures were simply defending themselves from a perceived threat.

Once, while fly-fishing with Carmen at a lovely trout stream, I happened to step on or very near the underground nest of yellow-jackets. Had my attention not been upon a native trout I saw hovering beneath a partially submerged log, I might have noticed the comings and goings of yellow-jackets from an inch-wide hole in the ground. Apparently, the "intruder alarm" was broadcast and hundreds of yellow-jackets began buzzing around my head. I've been told that yellow-jackets instinctively try to sting between the eyes of a trespasser. At least two were successful in that endeavor. The attack was so sudden and the swarming so disorienting that I just stood there waving my arms for a moment. Carmen yelled for me to run. After I had distanced myself by nearly a thousand feet from the nest, the yellow-jackets gave up the chase. I consider myself fortunate to have been stung only a dozen times.

There is much more to know about wasps, hornets, and bees. Their habits and even their defense methods are as various as they are interesting.

Anaphylactic Shock

If you or anyone in your crew knows they have a severe allergy to bee stings then everyone old enough to properly handle an EpiPen or other epinephrine auto-injector should be aware of the allergy, should know where to find the epinephrine auto-injector, and should be shown precisely how to use it.

Problematic Plants

Before setting out into weedy or brush-filled areas it is wise to be able to recognize at least some of the plants you might encounter - particularly those that can cause you or your crew great discomfort.

Poison Oak, Poison Ivy and Poison Sumac

Among the more commonly found plants that you would not want to touch are: poison oak, poison ivy, and poison sumac. The leaves of each of these plants hold oils that can create extremely itchy rashes on exposed skin. Poison oak is mostly found in the far west of the continental United States. Poison ivy can be found almost anywhere in the United States. By comparison, poison sumac has a relatively limited dispersal. I strongly suggest that you become very familiar with and can readily recognize whichever of these plants you might find where you intend to camp.

For both poison oak and ivy there are people who will recite the old rhyme, "Leaves of three, let it be." Although both plants normally do exhibit leaves in groups of three, so do wild strawberries, emerging Virginia creeper (although the mature ones have five leaves,) certain briers, and countless other plants. Thus, the old rhyme can be misleading. It is far better to read and to view the particular characteristics of each plant you want to avoid so that you will recognize it the moment you see it.

Although I have had my share of problems with poison oak, my main experience is with poison ivy. The most problematic aspect of poison ivy is that it can appear in many different forms. It can be a low plant that is often less than a foot tall. Poison ivy can also become a shrub or even a vine. There also is what some folks call a "witch's tree," referring to any tree that harbors poison ivy as a vine, the tendrils of which may hang down low enough to brush against one's face. Add to all of this that, depending upon the time of year and/or temperatures, poison ivy leaves may appear as a deep, bright green, a soft yellow, or even a shade of red. In all instances, the leaves are at least somewhat shiny and have sparsely notched edges. But there is one more form in which poison ivy may appear.

As a child I loved to climb trees. I once came upon a large oak, the first branch of which was much too far from the ground for me to reach. As luck would have it, there were huge, thick vines covering the face of the tree that could work as handholds and footholds that I could use to get to that first branch. I noticed that the vines were somewhat hairy-looking and that the "hairs" were of a somewhat rusty red color. Everything went as planned and I soon attained a perch upon that first branch. I suppose it was two or three days later that the rash first appeared. It began as just a few groups of very small bumps. It was not more than a day later that the little bumps became small blisters. I cannot begin to tell you all of the places the rash appeared nor do justice in describing how itchy all of it was. I can only tell you that I was quite miserable for about two weeks.

I think it is fair to say that one feature of poison ivy is that the more often you are exposed to it, the more severe your reaction is likely to be. For some people the reverse may also be true. I have successfully avoided contacting poison ivy for so long that even when I do accidentally brush against some of it, I barely get a rash. There are some people who can somehow exhibit no reaction at all to poison ivy even after deliberate handling of the plant. I have to wonder how many exposures it might take to break down that resistance. On the other end of the spectrum I have known people who would develop a rash just by being in the vicinity of someone mowing or weed-eating an area containing poison ivy.

One other important thing to note about poison ivy is that you should never, ever burn it. Inhaling the smoke can cause severe irritation to the throat and lungs. This is another reason to be careful when collecting "dead and down" firewood.

Thorns, Needles, and Other Irritations

Although most thorny plants aren't particularly poisonous it is well worth mentioning a few here. Enumerating the various varieties of thorny plants could take up a lot of pages. The most obvious member of the group is cactus. Now, I will need to admit that there was a time long ago when I believed that only people in the western USA needed to worry about encountering cactus plants. When I thought of cactus, I pictured the elbowed Saguaro cactus of western movie fame or else the barrel cactus that saved a thirsty soul in other movies of the same kind. You can imagine that I was surprised to learn that there is no state in any of the United States in which cacti cannot be found growing both naturally and cultivated.

Most of the cacti found east of the Mississippi River are fairly low to the ground. They favor sunny, well-drained areas and can sometimes even be found hanging from meager footholds on ledges or in the cracks of a rock face. At first glance you might not recognize the extremely small, dark clumps on a "blade" of cactus as holding tiny needles. You may even be attracted to the cacti by the dainty, bright yellow or red flowers. But beware! The tiny thorns or needles are there and will not only stab your skin but also will break off from the plant. The needles of those cacti are so small that some kinds of tweezers are just too bulky to grasp the needles well enough.

The stinging nettle is another plant to avoid because even brushing against a stinging nettle will release the tiny, stiff hairs of the plant. The stinging nettle's hairs, when in contact with bare skin, can cause considerable discomfort that is said to be similar to thousands of tiny ants stinging all at once.

Virtually anyone who has ventured into a wooded area has encountered briers. Briers are the long, usually green, thorny, and somewhat leafy branches that seem to suddenly appear out of nowhere. From a respectful distance a brier is actually somewhat graceful in appearance and its heart-shaped leaves are often so beautifully green and the young leaves, so shiny. It is usually when you encounter briers unawares that the trouble begins. Their thorns seem to grasp your clothing and most certainly can puncture or tear at your skin. Most of the time I have been able to release their hold by turning my body in the opposite direction from that of the thorns. The brier's thorns usually point toward the thicker part of the branch. It doesn't take long to figure out which way to turn, though, because if you don't do it right you are rewarded by having the thorns dig more deeply into your clothing or skin.

It is important to teach small children about briers because if they were to panic when "attacked" by a briery branch they would more than likely entangle themselves even more as they attempted to fight their way out.

Edibles vs. Inedibles

Most people love freshly picked berries. A wide variety of wild berries become available during the warmer months, most of which are not only edible, but also delicious. Some folks also enjoy certain other of Nature's gifts such as some particular greens that are useful in salads or as cooked vegetables. There are also wild mushrooms to be had for those who can safely identify them.

It is extremely important that children learn that only certain ones of the many growing things one can find in the wild are safe to eat. Kids need to be taught that not all berries are edible for humans even though squirrels and other animals might find certain berries quite tasty. Children should know that some plants or parts of plants can make anyone terribly, terribly sick. Kids should also know that only certain special mushrooms are the ones that won't make a body sick or might even kill them.

It is worth noting that ripe berries attract quite a broad variety of critters. Rodents are among the animals that berries might attract. Many kinds of snakes enjoy snacking on rodents. Just keep a careful eye out for them as you gather those yummy treats.

CAMPGROUND MANNERS

A campground is usually a comparatively small community compared to those in which most people live. Because of a campground's compact size, the need for good manners and respect for the privacy of others becomes magnified in inverse proportion. If you do some quick math considering that there could be an overall average of three campers per campsite and possibly thirty or more sites per camp loop, it means you might have at least ninety other campers within "shouting distance" of your campsite. In some tightly packed campgrounds even a quietly spoken word can be heard by nearby neighbors. Thus, it often can be quite challenging to maintain your own privacy; much less, the privacy of your neighbors. This is most especially true where children and/or dogs are a part of the scene.

Boundaries

A person's campsite is, in effect, their home and land, no matter how temporary. In most cases they have paid for the rent of that small area and as such they consider it as their own for the length of their stay. As it is with any other property upon which someone makes their home, friends are welcome; but strangers must be invited or at minimum must announce their presence and politely state their purpose.

It is bad manners to invade someone else's campsite.

If you bring children to the campground watch them carefully - especially for the first day or so - until they become aware of their new surroundings and of rules that might not be familiar to them. Please be sure they understand the boundaries of your campsite as well as proper etiquette regarding the campsites of others. This is especially important to note if a campsite should happen to be near a bathroom. Unless otherwise directed, children (and many adults) often will travel the most direct route to a bathroom or to any other destination without consideration of boundaries.

Some things that may seem obvious to adults are not necessarily seen that way by children. This is particularly true with regard to potential consequences of their actions. If they are sent out to gather firewood it may need to be pointed out that the firewood on other people's campsites is out-of-bounds. Kids may not readily recognize that thrown rocks, baseballs or other hard objects might not land where intended, possibly causing injury or equipment damage to nearby campers. Usually after the first day or so of camping children become accustomed to recognizing boundaries and other limitations.

Noise

Something I have seen far more often than I would like is that there are far too many very self-centered, inconsiderate campers who have no regard whatsoever for how their actions might interfere with the enjoyment of others around them. Some of those actions may be done out of ignorance, but many are not so easily excused.

Loud Music

Let me say at the outset that I have had a love affair with music for my entire life. But for those who camp in order to enjoy the peacefulness of nature, there are few things more disruptive than music blaring from a nearby campsite. Included among the offenders are those who play loud music as they drive through the campground. By what logic can it be assumed that anyone else wants to hear it in that venue - even if by some miracle the choice of musical styles coincidentally matches that of the neighbor? Yet anyone who has ever camped in almost any kind of campground has found themselves victimized by some thoughtless camper who imposed his musical taste upon anyone and unfortunately everyone in the area.

Car Horns

I doubt that anyone who reads this would have any uncertainty whatsoever that car horns are not directional. The sound of a car horn cannot be confined to only the hearing of the person to whom it is supposedly directed. Maybe in some environments (although I cannot think of any) honking a car horn is an appropriate method for calling children from play to a meal or some such. But the only honking I would want to hear while camping would be that of a passing flight of geese.

Quiet Hours

Nearly every campground posts a schedule that specifies "quiet hours." Most children and some adults need to have advance warning of the approach of the quiet time so they can begin to ramp down any loud or boisterous activities. During "quiet hours" is possibly the very best time to break out the marshmallows or to serve the apple crisp or to settle the kids with some quiet activities.

Generators

In many campgrounds there are clearly posted indications of when and even where RV generators may be run. In some campgrounds the use of free-standing generators is prohibited. If you plan to use a generator while camping it is your responsibility to make yourself aware of any and all restrictions and to abide by them.

PETS

Your dog or cat can easily become overwhelmed by the new environment at camp. All might go smoothly at home; but the picture could change quite drastically if pets are confined to an RV or are simply attempting to understand their new surroundings at a campsite. Pets other than cats or dogs are usually only regulated under state or federal laws but still may require some consideration as to whether life at camp is suitable to the pet's needs and habits.

Dogs

Many campgrounds have areas designated for campers with dogs. Among those there are also some that have very specific rules about where those dogs are allowed to be walked. It is wise to learn and understand those restrictions when you consider bringing your dog along on your camping adventure.

Nearly every campground has rules about keeping dogs on leashes. Often the length of the leash is also specified. Some dog owners ignore leash requirements because they feel very confident of their dog's ability to stay close at hand and under control by way of voice commands. However, the distant crunching of leaves by a squirrel or a deer might be just the trigger to set your dog running to investigate. New smells can have the same effect. As a general rule, campground or park employees have more than enough to do than to form a search party to find your missing dog. That is not to say they won't make the effort; but the necessity for a search is something that easily could be prevented through the use of a leash.

Dogs bark. That's not news, is it? Most dog owners know there are various kinds of barks that signal different things. Barking may indicate hunger or excitement. Most dogs will bark when they detect another dog's presence in order to make that other dog aware of the barking dog's existence and/or territory. Many dogs perceive that they have a duty to protect you from danger. Your dog's first line of defense is to bark at anything they consider to be a threat. If some other distant dog has noted a threat, your dog may feel compelled to "sound the alarm." Before you know it every dog within barking distance is either spreading the news or letting the other dogs know of a territorial claim.

At home your dog may normally only rarely bark and is easily quelled when it does. However, there are hundreds of new sounds at a campground, any of which can bring about a barking response. If it ended there that would be no problem at all. You tell your dog that everything is okay, assuring it that there is no threat. The problem is that one dog's barking can set off a chain reaction of dogs, such as mentioned above, causing a very disruptive event. I believe they are saying to each other, "I'm over here! Don't come too close or there might be trouble!"

I know of few remedies for keeping a dog from barking. Perhaps among the better methods are distractions. Many dogs can become so distracted by a new toy or by something very chew-worthy that they will focus almost entirely upon such offerings. RV owners can sometimes find that putting your dog inside (so long as you are outside and nearby) can also be effective. I believe that manner of separation may somewhat relieve the dog of feeling it is "on duty."

Cats

Fortunately, cats don't bark. In fact, with a few notable exceptions, they are generally quiet. However, they can be at least as susceptible to the intrigues of new surroundings as their canine counterparts. Although most campgrounds' rules are aimed specifically at dogs and their owners, cat owners should also always keep their felines on leashes when the cats are outdoors.

I know of a gentleman who had what he thought of as being a well-trained cat. He brought her out of his RV to a food dish he had prepared and had set upon the picnic table. The cat ate a little of the food while the man finished setting up camp. Moments later when he looked again the cat was gone. The man called and called, searched and searched. The campground staff also looked for the missing cat. Ultimately, the gentleman extended his stay at the campground for a number of days in an attempt to find his lost cat. Unfortunately, the animal was never again located or recaptured.

Again, new surroundings can be quite disorienting to a dog or cat and every precaution should be taken to ensure their safety. Pets such as dogs and cats can be at risk in the wild. They can become prey to any number of predators, including coyotes or mountain lions. A lost pet could accidentally encounter a poisonous snake. If you love your dog or cat you owe it to them to keep it safely on a leash.

Other Pets

Some other pets can greatly interfere with the camping enjoyment of others. The voices of some birds, parrots and magpies for instance, can be extremely obnoxious at times, their voices carrying far beyond a single camping space. As a general rule, most caged pets such as the aforementioned, as well as pythons, canaries, iguanas, and gerbils should remain at home or should at least be kept inside a climate-controlled RV for their own protection.

It is unfortunately very unlikely that any pet would ever be found if it somehow got out of its owner's control. It is even less likely that the lost pet would survive for very long in its new surroundings.

A FEW THINGS AN RVer SHOULD KNOW ABOUT CAMPING

Getting Your Rig Ready

The owner of a "pop-up" camper arrived at his campsite and began setting up. He, his wife, and two small children had just completed a three-hour drive and were already tired from the efforts spent in getting everything and everybody packed. After chocking the pop-up's wheels, the man began to turn the crank handle to the winch that raised the camper. A second or two later a loud pop let him know that his trials were not nearly over. The winch's cable had snapped. He was now unable to open his pop-up to make use of the sleeping quarters or even to retrieve some of the items stored within.

Fortunately, as camp host for that area at the time, I soon became aware of the problem. A quick inspection showed that the cable had rusted completely through at the point of the break. After some time, I was able to locate assistance through which a cable clamp was located and installed to enable the pop-up to be used normally.

On a different occasion an RV owner arrived at camp and after having set up camp he turned on his refrigerator. This was done moments before he and his wife were planning to leave camp to go to a local store to purchase food for a weekend of camping. Almost immediately smoke began to pour out of the refrigerator's outside vents. Seconds after that there were flames.

It happened that this occurred just a few campsites away from where Carmen and I were set up as camp hosts. Upon seeing the smoke, I grabbed a fire extinguisher and ran to be of assistance while Carmen notified emergency personnel. With some difficulty I managed to get the fire out, but only a few minutes before the fire trucks arrived. Luckily, although the refrigerator was ruined, there was very little other damage. It turned out that the refrigerator was set to run on propane and the burner's vent had most likely become blocked by a wasp nest or by bug carcasses.

In both of these instances the RVs had been unused since the previous camping season. Neither RV had seen proper maintenance at the end of the previous season's use. Nor had either RV been set up and inspected just prior to the current use to ensure that all systems were operating properly. In addition, steps had not been taken to ensure that all necessary lubrication had been performed.

Maintenance

A recreational vehicle of any kind requires regular maintenance as well as the very watchful eye of its well-informed owner. The observational powers of the RVs owner are greatly dependent upon the owner's understanding of the RVs various features and systems. Without an extensive and thorough knowledge of their RV an owner can neither perform preventive maintenance nor properly understand how their actions or negligence might actually damage the RVs equipment.

Reading owners' handbooks and equipment manuals can be tedious. However, the rewards are often worth the effort. Not only can you keep yourself and your campmates from possibly causing harm to your rig, but knowing how to use, how to adjust, or perhaps even how to repair your equipment can save you money.

There are some wonderfully educational resources online for those who camp in recreational vehicles. Through online videos you can find answers to nearly any question you may have about the functions of RV systems, including how electrical, drinking water, and sanitary systems operate. There are also video instructions on proper maintenance practices, many of which you can do yourself. My favorite resource for RV maintenance ideas and answers is called, "RV Education 101."

Backing

So, you have finally decided to purchase a pull-behind camper. It might be a small pop-up or could be a huge "fifth-wheel." Whatever it may be, don't wait until you leave to head for the campground before you check to see how everything works and how to steer your rig when backing. Practice backing into your driveway or into a parking space at a wide-open area of a large parking lot. Backing a pull-behind can be challenging and sometimes absolutely difficult.

Most campgrounds are designed to make the parking process as easy as possible, by angling the driveways or even by furnishing pull-through parking. However, many campground driveways are marked with stationary signposts and may even include a few trees that are not ideally placed. One thing that almost all campgrounds have in common is their jealously protected grassy strips that separate one campsite from another. The last thing you want is to destroy one of those grassy areas or to crunch into a post or tree as you fumble your way into your campsite. Also, you may not want to be the one to supply comic relief to all of the other campers around you. Trust me, they all will be watching.

If you are the driver and have a co-pilot or trusted friend with you, enlist their help in directing you. Before your helper begins assisting, you should mutually agree on hand signals even if you have a microphoned camera in the rear. You should establish that you, as the driver, will consider that all hand signals will refer to how to move the back end of the rig unless you are otherwise directed by word of mouth.

Never, ever make use of more than one helper. More directing will only serve to befuddle the driver. However, a helper will be of no use to the driver at all if he or she cannot be seen in the rear-view mirrors or their voices cannot be heard.

Before you begin backing roll down your windows and make certain the helpers know to stand where you can see and hear them. If you are blessed with a rear viewing camera, that can be of help as well but cannot be relied upon to the exclusion of all else.

If you do not have a reliable assistant then the backing process will necessarily involve your making small adjustments as you back and then getting out of your vehicle to check the result of that movement. If night has fallen before you begin parking your rig, placing a lit flashlight atop or next to a post or other obstruction can aid in avoiding possible collisions.

Perhaps one of the most important things to remember to do as you are backing is to make very small steering changes at a time. Over-correcting usually has the effect of begetting even more over-corrections. Back up a foot or so and watch what the rear of your rig does. If it seems to be heading in the right direction, all may be well. If not, turn the steering wheel a little in the opposite direction. It may be helpful to adopt the mindset that you are driving the pull-behind rather than pushing it. Whatever works for you is great; but the best methods won't come to you without practice. (See also the section on Generators in CAMPGROUND MANNERS.)

WEATHER

One of the most commonly overlooked components of camping is the weather. Weather can not only interfere to varying degrees with the enjoyment of camping, but it can also be dangerous. Yet countless people head out for parts unknown with little more than high hopes for great weather.

If there is to be scorching sun or pouring rain then a plan should include having a form of shady respite and/or quickly assembled shelter from the rain. Mountainous terrain is well known for unpredictable weather. Storms, sometimes serious ones, can form quite suddenly in the mountains. However, oncoming rainstorms viewed at some distance may be almost inexplicably deflected by mountain winds.

On the other hand, the occasional rain shower can make your adventure pleasantly unforgettable. If you are prepared with adequate rain gear to have a look around between showers you may find unexpected beauty. Wildflowers usually look their freshest after a shower of rain. Mushrooms often pop up not long after a rain. Certain kinds of rocks look particularly pretty when they are wet.

Rainstorms and Harsh Weather

Rainy weather can sometimes make camping - especially tent camping - difficult. It can be remarkably problematic if you have a leaky tent or if the downpour is so persistent that you are unable to cook a planned meal. I can honestly say that I have had very few camping adventures that were completely devoid of rain. For that reason, if for no other, preparations for foul weather should always be a part of planning.

If you have used your tent for more than a couple of seasons you ought to consider re-sealing the seams. You can find seam sealer in the camping section of many department or "big box" stores. It is usually easier to perform the re-sealing if the tent is set up. Many sealers apply more easily when used on a tent that has been warmed by the sun, but follow the directions on the sealer's label for best results.

A rainy day can interfere with meal plans unless forethought was given to such a possibility. A campfire or even the use of a camp stove can be rendered extremely difficult, at minimum, if not completely impossible. Planning should include at least a couple of just-in-case meals that can be put together with no cooking and as little effort as possible. Even so, food shouldn't ever be brought into your tent. To do so would be an invitation for ants, vermin, or even larger animals to invade your home away from home. A picnic in your vehicle might be the best alternative.

The occasions when, due to the weather, children are trapped indoors at home can be problematic, but children confined to just a few square feet of tent space can be trying not only for them but for others around them. It would be no great revelation to state that kids enjoy activity. Unless lightning strikes or falling trees or other such dangers are present then sufficient rain gear should be available to enable the kids to go out and play in the rain. They may form tiny dams for the runoff or just stomp a few puddles. Just so long as they don't dig any trenches or interfere with natural creek flow or something like that, they can find their own fun. But if your child can't go or doesn't wish to go out, then it is up to you to supply the means for activity. Did you bring a new or unread book for your child? When was the last time you took an opportunity to read to your child? Or perhaps your child might prefer to read to you. (See the section on KIDS for more ideas.)

It bears repeating that nearly every campground has regulations that prohibit trenching. If they don't, they should. Trenching is a method of diverting the flow of rainwater to prevent its flow toward a tent. The unfortunate result is that the water is forced to flow in an unnatural way that can often lead to erosion. Most campgrounds and managed forest areas take measures to ensure that designated campsites are well drained. However, trenching, on extremely rare occasions, may be necessary in some wilderness camping situations. If you must trench around your tent, before you leave be sure to replace the soil and pack it down to prevent erosion.

A sudden drop in temperature can be uncomfortable or even dangerous. It is always a good idea to have an extra layer of clothing at hand – especially when venturing a distance from camp. Hypothermia can be life-threatening.

Long ago I left camp without much more than a fly rod and a bottle of water. The part of the trout stream I wanted to fish was nearly an hour's walk away from camp. Between the time I started my first casts and the time I was almost halfway back to camp, the temperature dropped nearly 40 degrees. I was wearing a thin, long-sleeve shirt and jeans. By the time I got back to camp I was not only teeth-chatteringly chilled, but also found myself unable to think clearly. As soon as I arrived at camp I jumped into the car and ran it until the car's heater warmed me completely. I have never since been so ill-prepared for a change in the weather.

Some of the more obvious signs of hypothermia are: uncontrollable shivering, teeth-chattering, clumsiness, and impaired thinking. These symptoms may be followed by a reduced breathing rate, decreased heart rate, and may lead to death. Please be prepared for changes in weather.

HIKING

Taking a hike can be invigorating. If you take the time to notice your surroundings as you hike you will likely see some fascinating and beautiful aspects of the natural world. Depending upon the time of year and your location, there could be wildflowers, gorgeous butterflies, colorful birds, chipmunks, and deer. You might see enormous trees that could have been living when Thomas Jefferson was President. Every turn in the trail could present a memorable surprise.

Know Where You Are Going

Obtain a map of the trail or trails you are planning to hike. Your local supplier of backpacking needs will probably have what your need. There are also some very good resources online. Never rely solely upon a cell phone application or portable Global Positioning System (GPS) because terrain can greatly interfere with signal reception or even render reception completely unobtainable. If possible, discuss the trail with someone knowledgeable. They may be able to supply important information as to recent changes in the trail's route or might even suggest a better plan. Even if you have hiked the trail before you should always carry a map with you. Should you happen to need help for some reason, you can give whoever you send for assistance a map marked with your location. They, in turn, can plot the quickest route for finding help.

Let Someone Else Know Where You Are Going

Discuss your planned hike with a trusted friend who will not be going along or with a local ranger. Specify which trail you plan to take, any plans for camping along the trail, and when, at the very latest, you expect to return from your hike. If they don't already have one, give that person a copy of the map you intend to use, along with a listing of phone numbers for agencies to contact if you are inexplicably delayed. Among my family and friends, I've given them this information as I jokingly told them that this was where they'd need to look for the body.

In some areas you will need to obtain a permit to hike or in order to camp along a trail. Permits give you an additional measure of safety by way of your indication of your plans to the issuing agency. Be sure you notify whoever you have told of your hiking plans that you have returned from your hike. This will avoid unnecessary worry and might possibly even avert a search instigated by the interested parties.

Be Prepared

Plan for delays, unexpected weather, and for the possibility of injury. One of the attractions of hiking is not knowing what is beyond the next turn in the trail. While the unknown may bring pleasant surprises, conditions that could delay your hike may just as easily be just beyond the next turn of the trail. If, for instance, if a stream you need to cross has become too swollen to wade through where your trail leads, you may need to make use of an alternate route. Or you could find it necessary to seek refuge from a sudden storm for a while. Your progress might be slowed by the development of a blister on your foot. Delays like these are common and can sometimes greatly interfere with how long it takes for you to complete your hike.

Bring along more water than you think you'll need. It is extremely important to stay hydrated because doing so allows your muscles work more efficiently. On a hot day you could easily drink more than a pint per hour. Don't forget to have enough for your dog, if one accompanies you on your hike. An extra "energy bar" might prove to be a comfort for you if you are delayed. Some kibbles for your dog won't weigh down your pack, but would be very appreciated. A "space blanket," as those reflective Mylar sheets are known, can become very important if you become injured, must unexpectedly spend the night, encounter foul weather, or even need to signal your location on the trail.

Trail Markers

Be aware of trail markers. Many trails are marked at short intervals with "hash marks" or short stripes painted on trees or rocks. The color of the markings is important to note. Different colors are used to mark main trails, side trails, fire roads, or horse trails. As you hike, periodically check to ensure that the hash marks you see are of the same color as those you first encountered on the trail. Double hash marks normally indicate a sharp turn in the trail.

In some areas you might see trail intersections marked by four-sided, concrete posts or obelisks. Usually the posts will have metal bands attached near the top. The bands are embossed with names of trails, distances, and directional arrows. Read all four sides of the metal bands to be sure you know where you are and in which direction to head. One side of a typical band could read, "BRYCE ROCK 0.8 MI" followed by an arrow pointing which way to go. Other trail markers you might encounter are wooden signs that give similar information. However, many national and state parks have replaced wooden signs with more long-lasting markers because vandals sometimes destroyed or altered the wooden ones.

If you are making use of an unmarked trail that you plan to use as a return route, it may be wise to tie flagging tape at turns or trail intersections as you encounter them in order to mark your return route. Also, should an emergency arise, the ribbons will enable rescuers to find you more readily. As you make your way back to the trailhead please be sure to remove your ribbons. (Please see the section on

ROPE, CORD, STRING, WIRE, and TAPE for more information on the flagging tape.)

Food Storage

Backpackers who spend nights in trail shelters, in tents near the trail or in campgrounds must consider how to store their food safely. Bears and/or rodents are usually the biggest concerns, but raccoons and skunks can get into mischief as well.

Most trail shelters furnish "bear poles" but the shelters are better known by many hikers as havens for rodents. The mice and sometimes rats have been known to eat their way into backpacks in order to track down the residual scent of food that might have been carried. Some savvy backpackers purposely avoid camping at shelters because of the habitual presence of mice that are not only infamous for their investigative chewing, but also for the urine the mice leave behind. Mouse urine is connected with a number of serious diseases, perhaps the most common of which is called Hantavirus Pulmonary Syndrome. I have seen trail shelters where other hikers have left behind some rather cleverly designed anti-rodent hooks from which to hang backpacks. The majority of the clever devices are easily circumvented by hungry mice.

No matter where backpackers may choose to camp, their food should be contained in a separate bag that can be hung on a "bear pole," placed in a "bear box," hung from a tree limb, or kept in a bear-proof canister. The use of any of these food storage options is likely to prevent access by most wildlife. (Please also see the section on raccoons, squirrels, chipmunks, skunks, etc. in the WILDLIFE section as well as for more information about tree storage, bear-proof canisters, "bear poles," and "bear boxes.")

Hiking Goals

The most memorable hikes are usually the ones that lead to a reward or goal of some sort. Part of the reward of a quick, there-and-back hike, or of a hike on a loop trail, is simply returning to camp. While the return may be enough of a payoff for some adults, it might not be as much of a reward for kids. It is probably a good idea to have some kind of special treat or camp activity that a child might happily anticipate. Sometimes on a long hike a weary child might be reinvigorated by the anticipation of a reward at the end of the hike. Often adults are not much different.

A goal may come in the form of a hike's destination or purpose and is sure to vary among hikers. Some hikers may simply enjoy viewing the plant life or fauna along the trail and see getting back to camp as a sufficient goal. Others may think that hiking to a breathtaking view from a rocky prominence would be a fine opportunity for some great photographs. Birdwatchers might enjoy the chance to encounter a particular species that may not be seen at other altitudes or in other climates. Waterfalls are some of the most popular hiking destinations. Waterfalls are favored because of their refreshing beauty and as being wonderful subjects for snapshots.

The main problem I have seen with most waterfalls hikes is that the majority of them involve almost exclusively downhill travel in order to get to the falls. What that means is that virtually all of the return routes must necessarily be uphill. Hiking uphill, especially on a hot summer's day is not something that most kids or out-of-shape adults would enjoy. My advice is to take downhill waterfalls hikes in the early morning after a very quick breakfast or with a plan for a breakfast on the trail. Other hikers are then less likely to be on the trail early. You may even see more wildlife in the morning and wildflowers will often be at their height of beauty at that time. In addition, if the return route is likely to be strenuous, the cooler part of the day would make the effort more pleasant. Some waterfalls can be accessed by way of a trail that begins below the falls. If that option is available, it would mean that the return route would almost certainly be downhill all the way!

WILDLIFE

Roy Rogers and his sidekick, Gabby Hayes, made a recording long ago that was filled with advice on how to be a cowboy. Among the wisdom they imparted was their admonishment, "Don't bother nothing that don't bother you." In other words, if you should happen to encounter some manner of wildlife while camping or hiking, you should observe and not interfere with it if at all possible. Most campgrounds were originally carved out of an area in which a variety of wildlife roamed freely. It was and, in many cases, still continues to be their home. You and other campers are in a sense invading the homeland of these creatures. In light of this it should make sense for you to let the wildlife do whatever they might normally do. Of course, if the presence of an animal in your camp will greatly interfere with your activities, your safety, or your enjoyment, then you should notify a camp staff member who will take the necessary action or will contact the appropriate authorities. The troublesome wildlife will be removed and will usually be relocated to a more suitable area.

I will not attempt to cover all of the animals that may disrupt or possibly even enhance your camping experience. Wild horses, feral pigs, and moose come to mind. As I have said elsewhere it is important for you to be aware of what wildlife may be in the vicinity of the area where you intend to camp. Many state and national forest campgrounds have full-color posters on display that indicate species that you could encounter in the area. Make note of them and plan how you might react if you were to meet up with any of those animals.

Bears

There are numerous areas in the United States where bears reside. Many of those areas include within them one or more campgrounds. In campgrounds where bears are commonly seen there are usually posted warnings about the potential for bears' presence and the precautions you should take. Pay close attention to these notices because they may differ according to what variety of bears inhabit the area.

Bear attacks on humans are infrequent and yet well worth noting. Some such attacks result in fatalities. In some instances, it was the human's reaction to the bear's presence or a lack of caution that provoked attack. However, some bears are more inclined to attack than others, sometimes simply because of their perception that the bear's territory has been invaded.

The American black bear is the most common bear in the United States. Black bears are found throughout much of the Eastern U.S. as well as in the Rocky Mountain region, in coastal Alaska, and in parts of the upper Midwest with a few small populations scattered in some areas of the Ohio Valley. They prefer densely wooded areas where human contact is less likely. Despite their name, black bears can have fur that ranges from nearly white to shades of brown and can even sometimes be found with blotches of these colors along with their more common, coal black coat.

In Virginia's Shenandoah National Park, the American black bear is the only kind of bear to be found. Because the park is almost completely surrounded by either mostly cleared farmland or by even more populated areas, the bear population lives in a virtually closed environment. Most of the bears living in that park have learned to peacefully coexist with the humans who frequent the park. For more than seventy-five years the park management there has kept a watchful eye upon the bears. The park rangers routinely relocate any bears that become too friendly with the humans or otherwise demonstrate the potential for unpleasant interactions. This is likely the reason that nearly all of the bears viewed there are mainly seen doing little more than going about normal bear activities rather than robbing picnic baskets as the cartoon bears do.

Black bears are generally somewhat more docile than many other species. They are usually more likely to move away from a human than to attack. This is not to say that black bears are harmless! A black bear can easily kill a human if provoked or if some other force - especially the deprivation of food - is part of the picture. Unlike many other bears, a black mother bear and cubs poses only a little more danger than any other black bear. However, attacks by female bears with cubs are not unheard of.

Historically, black bear attacks are often the result of the removal of a food source. Or an attack may have been preceded by a curtailment of the feeding of bears by tourists - something that should be (and likely is) prohibited everywhere. This is not to say that food is the basis for all attacks. Not often, but sometimes, a bear might attack if it thinks is territory is being invaded. It is believed by some that the number of reported black bear attacks is high due to the proportion of black bear population compared to that of other species.

Most reports of black bear attacks do not actually indicate a physical contact. Black bears will typically initiate a false charge of a few feet toward their perceived threat. They may huff, snort, or even growl. They may stand on their hind legs to get a better look and possibly to appear larger than what they may see as a potential foe. Then they usually wait to see what reaction their bluff and bluster might bring. What to do in this situation will be discussed later.

Brown bears, a species that includes grizzly bears and Kodiak bears, live in the upper Northwest of the United States. The Alaska brown bear lives mainly along the coast of Alaska. Grizzly bears can be found in Alaska, Washington, Idaho, and Montana although sightings have been reported in some nearby states.

Kodiak bears, not surprisingly, are found on or near Kodiak Island, Alaska. Brown bears are most easily distinguished from black bears by the brown bear's larger size and by a hump found just behind their heads. Brown bears are much more territorial than black bears and are therefore much more likely to cause serious problems for humans who happen to be in the wrong place at the wrong time.

The kind of bluffing mentioned above is not usually in the brown bear's repertoire. A brown bear's action is usually much more direct, charging almost immediately at any interloper, whether it is another bear or even a human - especially if the seizing of food or a food source is perceived as being threatened.

Most bears share certain attributes. The majority have acutely good hearing. Many bears' eyesight is about as good as or even better than a human's except that their distance vision may not be quite as effective. The distance vision problem might explain why bears sometimes need to stand on their back legs to get a better view or scent of something they can't see well. All bears have nearly incredible sense of smell, enabling them to detect food from more than a mile away. There are some reports of bears locating food more than five miles distant. They have excellent memories, especially when it comes to remembering food sources. Despite their awkward-looking gait bears can run quite fast, are good swimmers, and can climb trees.

It is bears' sense of smell to which campers in bear-populated areas must pay strict attention. Depending upon the kind of bear, its disposition, and most particularly its degree of hunger, your food or things of yours that a bear might suspect could be food can create some serious situations.

Bears and some other creatures might consider the scent of certain toiletries as possibly being food. Toothpaste and even some hand creams can attract their attention. (Please see the section on Raccoons, Squirrels, Chipmunks, Skunks, Etc. for food storage suggestions.)

Bear Encounters

The best way to avoid bear encounters is to give them advance warning of your presence. Sing a song or clap from time to time as you travel along a path. If you have others with you talking loudly can be helpful. Devices such as "bear bells" may also be useful.

Upon sighting a bear, the current recommendation is to not turn and run, but to back away slowly. If you are accompanied by one or more people, bunch tightly together as you exit the area. Try to refrain from looking directly into the eyes of the bear because the bear can sometimes perceive this as threatening. In some situations, such as encountering a bear at close range, it can be useful to try to look much bigger than you are by spreading your jacket and/or holding it open over your head or to raise your backpack in the same way. Shouting such things as, "Get away, bear!" in the gruffest voice you can manage can also be useful. Never scream or whistle or blow a whistle because these can be perceived by the bear as indications of helplessness and/or fear. Some hikers carry a pocket-size (about 1 oz.) air horn that has been found to be effective.

Any venture into bear country should include the carrying of a can of pepper spray that is specifically designed to use to repel bear attack. Read the instructions carefully, know how to disengage the safety catch if it has one, and most importantly, carry it where it can be readily accessible. Bear sprays have a limited range, beyond which they cannot project. A suggested strategy is to create a cloud of spray between you and the bear rather than to attempt to direct the spray into the face of an attacking bear.

As mentioned above, a bear (especially a black bear) might huff, pop their jaws, swipe at the ground, or even make a false charge. It is vital even then to remember to not run, but to continue backing away. If your precautions and actions fail then you should protect your face and head as much as possible. Do not drop to the ground nor assume a fetal position as was advised some years ago. You might only suffer a swat or two rather than a full-on attack. Bears are deceptively fast runners. You cannot outrun a bear. Do not attempt to seek refuge in a tree. Nearly all bears are excellent climbers.

Mountain Lions (Cougars, Pumas, Panthers), Lynxes (Bobcats), Feral Cats

Mountain lions are known by dozens of names. Although often associated with the western states they are well known in Florida and have been reported in such disparate places as Missouri and Massachusetts. Encounters with mountain lions are rare in most areas of the United States. Though they usually avoid direct contact with humans within their environments, mountain lions are documented to be in close proximity to people at times.

Mountain Lion Encounters

The most common encounters with mountain lions are accidental. If you happen upon a partly eaten deer carcass or one that is partially buried you should leave the area immediately. Deer are a mountain lion's favorite food and a lion may think you are going to interfere with its kill if you get too close. A number of resources currently advise that if you see a mountain lion you should quickly try to appear bigger. Raise your arms and waive them slowly. Bunch together with your fellow hikers or spread your jacket. If you have a dog with you leash it in closely. Act aggressive. Maintain eye contact. Make noise. Yell, bang your walking sticks together. Whatever else you do, don't bend down or squat - even if it is to lift a child into your arms or to pick up a rock to throw. Just don't do it. Don't run. Stand your ground or else back away slowly. The main thing is to convince the lion that you aren't prey. If you are attacked despite these efforts you should protect your neck and make use of any means you can (rocks or sticks or even bare hands) to deter the lion.

Lynxes (of which bobcats are a subspecies) are even less often known to attack humans. They are small, rarely exceeding 40 pounds, but more commonly weigh less than 10 pounds, depending upon habitat. Their range extends throughout the continental United States, but they are rarely seen. Their favored food is rabbit but will eat any small animal - even crickets or grasshoppers. Attacks on humans are virtually unheard of. However, small dogs should be leashed at all times to reduce the likelihood of their being attacked.

Feral cats are usually quite secretive and are rarely a problem to campers. These cats may be attracted by food scraps or unattended pet food. It is best to keep your distance from feral cats.

Raccoons, Squirrels, Chipmunks, Skunks, Etc.

Nearly everyone considers what to do when in bear country, but they don't give much thought to the smaller critters. Raccoons, squirrels, chipmunks, rats, mice, and certainly skunks can cause some major problems. For these animals as well as for nearly any animal, the search for food is their main occupation. You only have to discover a hole chewed through your expensive tent just once to appreciate how problematic some of the smaller animals can be.

At the risk of repeating something said elsewhere in this book: Never, ever store food or anything that may be considered to be food in your tent! Such things as toothpaste, certain cosmetics, and chewable vitamins can smell like food to many animals. Watch your children carefully to be sure they don't sneak any candy or leave any candy wrappers in your tent.

Of course, a plastic container or cooler on the picnic table would be little challenge for many critters. Some of the ones that couldn't easily pry off the lid could simply knock the container onto the ground to spread out the contents for access. But some other animals might take a more direct route and chew a hole in a container to reach the food inside.

Do you really want a skunk in your camp? If not, it would be wise to check under the picnic table and all around the camp to see if any food has accidentally been dropped onto the ground. What about the trash? Surely, you're not going to leave that trash bag hanging only a foot or so off the ground! Take it to the dumpster or store it safely. Because campground staff are well acquainted with the local wildlife, they will most probably supply you with instructions as to how best to store your food and what to do with your trash.

Please keep in mind that some animals may be attracted by the scents of toothpaste, some hand creams, and other toiletries. It is best to store toiletries of those kinds as you would your food.

If you are backpacking and taking advantage of a stay at a campground you may be faced with other considerations. You shouldn't leave food within your pack - especially if you intend to keep your pack in your tent. When you register for a campsite in bear country ask if there are campsites that are furnished with "bear boxes" or if the campground has a "bear pole" somewhere. "Bear boxes" are usually metal cabinets with latches designed to keep out bears as well as smaller creatures.

A "bear pole" is a tall metal post from the top of which extend metal rods. The "bear pole" is handier and more effective than using a tree upon which to hang your food bag. Bear poles are too slick for a bear to climb and the metal rods keep the food bags too high for a bear to reach. If you have never used a "bear pole" look on or near it for a metal rod to use for lifting your food bag onto the aforementioned rods.

If neither a bear box or a bear pole is available then making use of a tree may be almost your only choice. The recommendation is to hang your food bag at least ten feet off the ground and at least four feet from the trunk of the tree where the branch is unlikely to be sturdy enough for a full-grown bear's weight. Experienced backpackers usually carry not only a long rope but also a pulley to make this process much easier. Because there may be other hungry critters around besides bears, it is a good idea to dangle the food bag at least three feet below the branch.

Another option is to bury packages of food in scattered locations at least 50 feet away from where you will be camping. By distributing the food in this manner, the bears or other creatures are unlikely to find all of it and you will still have something remaining for you to eat.

In addition, there are commercially sold, bear-proof canisters for food storage. There are some areas where the use of the canisters is strictly required.

Keep in mind that the safekeeping of your food is paramount to the enjoyment, if not the duration, of your camping experience.

Snakes

Please note that for the purposes of this discussion I will use the terms "poisonous" and "nonpoisonous" as general categories. The snakes whose bites are toxic can be classified as either "venomous" (meaning they have means for injecting poison) or "poisonous" (meaning that they secrete toxins.) There are some snakes in the world that carry both labels. For the sake of simplicity, I will use the most commonly used designation of all snakes that can deliver toxins by any means as being "poisonous."

Most people don't like to be around snakes. I won't go into the many possible reasons for that fear, but will simply say that people have felt that way for thousands of years. Likewise, most snakes prefer not to be around people. People tend to walk around a lot, creating lots of vibrations that greatly interfere with a snake's ability to detect the approach of prey. Not only that but the presence of people also can scare off or at least alter the behavior of a snake's preferred foods. However, occasionally a snake will inadvertently wander onto someone's campsite, usually while the snake is on the way to someplace else entirely. Because a snake's hearing essentially consists of sensing vibrations through their contact with the ground, if nobody in camp has moved for a while, a passing snake may not even be aware of anyone's presence.

Years ago, I was at a friend's somewhat remote home, building a doghouse. I was intent upon measuring and marking a piece of plywood for cutting and so had stood in one place for quite some time. Just as I was about to make a cut with a power saw and was checking for possible obstructions, I saw some movement out of the corner of my eye. It turned out that a copperhead was rapidly weaving its way down a slight grade and directly toward where I stood. Realizing that the snake was completely unaware that I was in its path I had the presence of mind to stomp my feet. That brought the copperhead to a full stop. It immediately coiled into a defensive position, with most of its head hidden among the coils. The snake began to sample the air with its tongue in an attempt to discover whether the vibrations might indicate some sort of danger.

This sort of behavior is fairly typical of most snakes. People sometimes believe that a snake might be coming toward them as some kind of attack when the snake may very well not even know the person is there.

One other important aspect of snake behavior is that most of them prefer to ambush their prey. It is extremely important to be aware of this behavior when in a rocky area containing many crevices. This preference for ambushing often entails a snake's hiding in some small nook or under an overhanging rock where it has a clear view of approaching prey but remains hidden from view. Concealment can serve the additional purpose of preventing attack by predators. Yes, snakes of all kinds can fall prey to other snakes or can be eaten by hawks, raccoons, roadrunners, rodents, coyotes, and a surprising number of other animals.

Like most animals, snakes have certain behavioral traits. Some of those demeanors have led to generalized reputations for predispositions. For instance, the eastern diamondback rattlesnake is often said to be quite aggressive while the copperhead is reputed to be far more docile. In my experience any snake can manifest a variety of behaviors, often in reaction to a particular situation or degree of molestation. In other words, a snake can become quite irritable for any number of reasons or can just as easily be in a mood to shrink away from a confrontation.

I dislike generalities but will risk saying that the default demeanor as well as posture of the majority of snakes is one of self-defense. When a snake senses danger it will coil in such a way as to protect its head while still allowing its tongue to taste the air and for its eyes to see any impending danger. Coiling, while allowing the snake to protect its head from attack, also affords the snake the ability to focus its muscular energies for the possible necessity of a strike against its perceived foe. Striking and biting except when capturing prey are normally used as final defense tactics and are often immediately followed by rapid retreat. When surroundings impair retreat, multiple strikes and/or bites can be expected.

It is important to know what kinds of snakes might inhabit the area in which you expect to camp. If it is possible that poisonous snakes might be in the vicinity then you should learn which ones they are and get a clear notion of their appearance or description. If you were to camp in say, New Hampshire, it is virtually impossible that you would encounter a cottonmouth water moccasin but in certain areas of the state you could see a timber rattlesnake. There are poisonous snakes in nearly all of the United States. Alaska is the only state in which no poisonous snakes have ever been recorded. Hawaii has no terrestrial poisonous snakes.

I mentioned cottonmouth water moccasins above. The three things that most people know about cottonmouth water moccasins are that they are poisonous, the insides of their mouths are white, and they probably can be found around water. While these bits of knowledge are true, the last item does not mean that any snake found in or near water is a cottonmouth water moccasin. Despite regulatory protections, hundreds of snakes of other species are killed each year simply because they were in or near water. I don't know of any snake that can't swim. Most can be readily recognized as something other than cottonmouths because the majority of other snakes, as they swim, are intent upon holding their heads out of the water while the rest of the snakes' bodies remain mainly underwater. Water moccasins usually swim very much on top of the water. In some areas, you might see a cottonmouth water moccasin all but bobbing like a cork as it lies motionless on top of the water. They float remarkably well.

Many people ask, "How do you know if a snake is poisonous?" Outdoorsmen and others who are familiar with snakes will glibly respond by saying that it is easy to tell the difference between poisonous and nonpoisonous snakes. "The shape of the head and of the eyes will tell you." they will say. From what I have seen among people who are fearful of snakes, it is not as easy as that. Most folks would prefer to be so distant from a snake as to have no idea as to the shape of the head, let alone the shape of the eye. Be that as it may, the self-proclaimed "experts" are not entirely accurate.

Although it is true that the majority of the poisonous snakes have roughly triangular heads and vertical pupils, the coral snake of the Deep South has neither attribute. The coral snake family has one readily identifying feature about its colorful members. If the snake's red areas or red rings are bordered by yellow or yellowish rings then it is definitely a coral snake. Remember this: **RED TOUCHES YELLOW - KILL A FELLOW.** Sadly, there are varieties of the non-poisonous king snake with markings that are, at first glance, quite similar to the coral snake except the colors are in a different order. Because of that similarity many of those beautiful king snakes are mistakenly killed.

In most instances, when a snake is within approximately three feet, it is best to try to remain in place. With some exceptions, three feet is usually thought of as the possible striking distance for most snakes. At that range most snakes can see movement. Most importantly, avoid any movement that could produce a vibration that the snake might feel and perceive as threatening. It may take a while, but once the snake is no longer aware of a threat, it will probably move on. It could be useful to teach your children to "freeze" just as they might do for a game of "freeze tag."

I have heard far too many people declare that "The only good snake is a dead one!" What they fail to recognize is that their fear of snakes is largely unfounded. For starters, only about fifteen percent of snakes can deliver venom, which I imagine is why folks fear them in the first place. Snakes perform an important role in the ecological system they inhabit. Most aid greatly in reducing the rodent population while others help to keep even smaller animals under control. For these reasons and more, in most state and national parks throughout the country it is prohibited to kill snakes of any kind. (Please see information on Snakebites in the GENERAL SAFETY section.)

Wolves, Coyotes, Wild Dogs, and Foxes

It is difficult to generalize about this group of animals except to say that most campers are unlikely to encounter any of them. Unless driven by an extreme scarcity of other food sources wolves will usually avoid interacting with humans. In all likelihood a camper may only be aware of the presence of any of these animals by hearing a signaling howl. Coyotes and foxes are normally very secretive. If they are in the area at all it would be little more than coincidental to catch sight of any of them, much less for either to be a problem. Wild dogs are rarely encountered and problems with them are uncommon. Stray dogs are far more common and would be the most likely of these to encounter while camping.

All members of what can broadly be termed as this family of animals are attracted by movement. Because wolves, coyotes, wild dogs, and foxes are fast runners, there is no instance in which it would be advisable for you to run from an encounter unless an extremely easily climbed tree is just a few steps away. Although some of these animals can jump high, none is particularly adept at tree climbing. However, I have seen some surprising exceptions. An aggressive animal can sometimes be distracted if an article of clothing such as a hat is proffered. Slowly backing away is usually best. Turning your back to make an exit is never a good idea because it is often perceived by most predators as an opportunity for attack. In most instances it is inadvisable to look the animal directly in the eye because this can trigger an escalation of aggression.

Flies, Wasps, Yellow Jackets, Ants, and Spiders

It is probably unrealistic to think that flies, wasps, and yellow jackets won't be present when food is on hand at your campsite. One of the best ways to deal with them is to distract them. Smear a small paper plate with jelly or honey and place it downwind at a distance from where you are eating. Most of the bothersome pests will then leave you in comparative peace. Be sure to dispose of the distracting plate after your meal is over.

Keeping the ground around your camp clear of dropped food will aid greatly in discouraging ants. However, if you discover a trail of ants headed to somewhere you don't want them, try sprinkling a little vinegar across their path. It will disorient them and may bring about a full retreat. I heard about one camper who kept a spray bottle of diluted vinegar for that purpose as well as for general cleaning.

It is virtually impossible to keep spiders from exploring your campsite. It is always good to be cautious when handling firewood that has been piled for a long time or when reaching into dark recesses of any kind because of the possibility that a poisonous spider, such as a black widow or brown recluse, might be hiding there. (Please see the section on GENERAL SAFETY for more information.)

Turtles, Frogs, Salamanders, and Crayfish

I cannot begin to count the hours I spent as a child wading in creeks or stalking ponds and capturing turtles, frogs, salamanders, crayfish, etc.. All of my captures were accomplished in sheer innocence and as the manifestation of a limitless curiosity about the world around me. Not one of the creatures was ever transported more than a few hundred feet from its natural home. I am happy to be able to say that, after a certain amount of careful examination, all of my captives were eventually allowed to return to their former environments.

Unfortunately, not everyone does the same with captured animals. Some people envision keeping the animals as pets, but have no idea of how to properly care for them. Others, usually small children, soon lose interest in their captives, but fail to return the creatures to the place of capture. It is at that point that an adult should guide the child to release the animal to its former location.

While I am a strong advocate of allowing anyone a closer look at the living treasures to be found in the wild, I sincerely believe that any capture should be followed by release as soon as possible afterward. Quick release to the animal's former habitat can reduce the potential for unintentional damage to the creature while demonstrating empathy and respect for a fellow inhabitant of this planet.

A Note About Animals

It is important to remember that many wild mammals are capable of carrying rabies. A rabid animal can exhibit unusual behavior or may become excessively aggressive. Attacks on humans are sometimes a result of an animal's becoming infected with rabies.

A wide variety of animals can also transmit a number of other unpleasant diseases and bacterial infections such as tetanus and tularemia. A bite from virtually any animal can cause serious illness.

Wild animals of all kinds deserve our compassion and our respect. When we camp, we have an opportunity to become, in some ways, temporary members of the animal community of that environment. In doing so we should recognize our fellow creatures must be held in high regard and must be allowed to go about their normal activities with as little of our interference as possible. It is more or less what we expect them to do for us. Shouldn't they be offered the same courtesy?

PESTS

One camping guide I've read states that the very worst pest at camp is the lazy camper. Because some parts of camping can be hard work, it is important that every member of the camping party participate in the tasks of setting up camp, meal preparation, and the packing away of camping equipment. By being a useful member of the crew, the other members can also enjoy the camping adventure.

Unfortunately, there are other pests that can sometimes interfere with the enjoyment of the outdoors.

Ticks

Ticks can be found throughout most of the United States and are particularly active during the warmer months. An important part of their life cycle is that they are unable to reproduce without having first feasted on a source of blood. A tick that has not become engorged by such a meal may range in size from the diameter of a small lima bean to a size smaller than a dot you might make with a pencil.

It is important to know that there are many varieties of ticks and that all can carry some very serious diseases. It is essential to check yourself and to encourage your crew check themselves for the presence of ticks. Although ticks seem to prefer the hairy regions of humans, they may also be found elsewhere such as where clothing is tight against the body. It can help to have a family member or intimate partner to aid in inspection.

There are numerous repellants available that are specifically designed to repel ticks. Some are far better than others. Your own research will guide you toward a suitable choice. Many outdoorsmen advise tucking your pantlegs into your socks as an effective deterrent against ticks. Most also indicate that one of the best uses of a repellant is to apply it to your socks. (Please see the section on FIRST AID KIT and MEDICATIONS for instructions for tick removal.)

Mosquitoes

Mosquitoes feed on blood. In order to do so they drill tiny holes in the skin of an assortment of animals, humans among them. To aid in their drilling they make use of a secretion that softens the tissues. It is this secretion that is the main cause of the itching that accompanies a mosquito bite.

Like most animals, the majority of mosquitoes do most of their feeding in the early morning and evening hours. In highly infested areas you may find them to be quite evident at nearly any hour.

Once I camped on a river bank where the mosquitoes were so thick that as they became attracted to the flames of the "canned heat" that was being used as lighting, they actually extinguished it! On a separate outing I decided to not use a tent. It had been a tiring day and I fell asleep soon after dark. When I awoke and had an opportunity to look into a mirror, I barely recognized the face I saw that was so distorted by swollen mosquito bites. Needless to say, both adventures would have been far more pleasant if some good mosquito repellant had been available.

Almost anyone you talk to has a notion as to what works best as a mosquito repellant. All sorts of creams, lotions, and oils are among the suggestions. However, in an article titled, "Mosquito Repellents That Best Protect Against Zika," (updated: June 27. 2017) appearing on the Consumer Reports.org website, was the statement, "The most effective products were those that contained 15 to 30 percent deet, 20 percent picaridin, or 30 percent OLE [oil of lemon eucalyptus]."

Preventing the mosquitoes' access to skin will always be the best deterrent. Full length pants and long-sleeve shirts are among the very best precautions when mosquitoes are present.

KIDS

There are few better gifts to give a child than to put them in touch with the outdoors. It is true, though, that some children simply may not enjoy the experience, but I believe kids should be given an opportunity to explore the camping environment. While school is still in session and particularly while you are working away from home you may have limited opportunities to meaningfully interact with your child. When you and your family camp you will likely have hundreds of chances to connect. They are precious times and are not to be squandered.

A camping adventure can be an excellent means for helping children to see themselves in a different context. They may not be the very best of students at school but while camping they may discover a knack for finding and identifying animal tracks or that they are great at learning how to cook at camp. On the other hand, you may make a few discoveries of your own. You might find that your child is virtually a genius at figuring out how to put up a screen tent. Your child might tell you something they read about butterflies that you never knew or might even create a miniature village out of nothing more than some rocks and a few sticks.

If you, yourself, are well acquainted with outdoor skills, hobbies, or crafts you owe it to your child to teach them some of what you know - but don't force it. You might, for example, offer to take your child fishing, but could receive a negative response. This may be a manifestation of a fear of the unknown or perhaps a revulsion having to do with the possibility of having to handle a fish or a worm. You might do well to just ask your child to accompany you and watch. Once they see how it can be done and that the handling of fish and worms is not a source for alarm, they may want to participate next time. On the other hand, something much simpler may be of interest. Perhaps just picking a few wild raspberries together might be fun - especially if a good many of them get eaten in the process. Plan alternatives.

One of the more important things to remember about bringing your child camping is to plan numerous options. A child who becomes bored is not likely to remember camping as an enjoyable experience. If the campground's swimming pool is shut down suddenly you should have a fun backup activity planned. A rainstorm might coincide with a hike you had intended to take. Have an alternative figured out just for that possibility. What if it rains heavily for quite some time? Think of what your family can do for fun while marooned within the tent or other shelter.

When such catastrophes strike is not the time to wonder. It is a time to reach into your "bag of tricks" and to come up with some pleasant activity you and your family can enjoy together. Maybe you had the foresight to bring along a deck of cards or a board game. This might be a great time for your kid to show you how to play that little electronic game he/she is forever messing with. Or maybe you can ask everyone to jump into the car so you can treat them all to ice cream at a nearby place you know. But what if you, clever person that you are, could produce a package you had secretly tucked away that has something within it that everyone will likely enjoy but have probably never attempted? While you are still in the planning stages of your camping trip, take time for a careful look through a crafts or hobby store. You just might encounter the very item needed to fill the bill.

This is not to say that every single moment should be filled with planned activities. Every member of the family should have a little time for themselves - an hour or two each day to do something on their own. Maybe somebody wants to just sit in the shade and read a book for a while. Someone else might want to snap a few photos, while someone else might feel a need to do some sketching. It is all part of the fun!

At first blush water balloons seem to be a great thing to supply for your kids on a hot, summer's day. Don't do it! Though the cooling splashes water balloons create may be just the thing to refresh overheated children, there is a problem: when a water balloon pops the remains of the balloon are left behind – and who would pop just one? They come in packages of 100 or even as many as 500! Imagine if you were to arrive at the campsite you reserved only to find it strewn with the multicolored remains of hundreds of water balloons a former camper left.

Unless you plan to spend an hour or two locating and picking up every single balloon scrap, they are simply a bad idea. Oh, wait. You don't seriously think the kids will do all that picking up for you, do you? Where's the fun in that?

The colorful balloon carcasses are very attractive to a variety of wildlife that may believe them to be food and can easily choke on them. Even if successfully swallowed, the item can also cause intestinal blockage. Either way a balloon can cause irreparable damage to an animal and can quite likely lead to their death. Until biodegradable balloons become available there are few, if any, places where it makes sense to use them and most especially not in a campground. (Please also see the section on Turtles, Frogs, Salamanders, and Crayfish regarding the capture and release of animals.)

LITTER

The paragraph I wrote about water balloons in the section on KIDS brings up the topic of litter. As a camp host who has often cleaned up picnic areas, beaches or campsites after their use, I consider myself somewhat an expert on litter. When I've picked up litter from any of those areas I did it with a single goal in mind: I wanted that area to be clean enough in appearance to give the next occupant the illusion of being the first to use them. Now, that may seem like a lofty goal, but I have been told time and again by campers how much they appreciated coming to such a clean campground.

Much of the litter I have encountered as a camp host has been unintentional. Lots of people and particularly children give little thought to whether something will become litter or that it might be blown onto someone else's campsite or picnic area. A parent hands a child one of those small box drinks, the sort that come with a little straw, and that's the end of it - or so they believe. What they may overlook is that those little straws come in clear, plastic wrappers that more often than not find their way to the ground. Of course, everybody knows how to open a bag of crackers or a candy wrapper - you just bite off one corner and then tear it open. Do you know what happens to that little corner that gets torn off? Yep, on the ground!

Have a look under and around almost any picnic table after a family meal and you are almost certain to find some litter. There's the napkin that escaped recapture. Over there is the chunk of hot dog that didn't quite make it to someone's mouth. Oh, and there's the missing plastic fork! Besides appearing messy, much of litter either is food or has food residue on it. Don't worry, a skunk will come to your campsite tonight to try to clean up what it can.

Admittedly, finding litter can sometimes be a challenge. Often such things as plastic wrappers, particularly the clear ones, will be invisible at first glance. Where there are fallen leaves, for instance, things similar in color to the leaves can nearly disappear. In many cases you'll need to view the area from various angles until you see the sun glinting off the plastic items. Other items just require looking very carefully.

Cigarette filters are the most common type of litter on the planet. In 1998 it was estimated that as much as 2.1 billion pounds of cigarette filters were discarded throughout the world. In an international survey and clearing of aquatic detritus, cigarette filters were the most common of all debris found. Smokers might be surprised to know that the filters are made of a form of plastic and as such will not readily decompose. Filters also contain chemicals that are hazardous to some animals. You can read more about this subject in an article that appeared in the August 2000 edition of *The Underwater Naturalist* called, "Cigarette Butt Litter" by Kathleen M. Register.

TRASH

As is mentioned elsewhere in this book, dumpsters or other trash receptacles are available in most campgrounds. At your camp, however, you will need to have brought a trash container to hold your daily refuse. The container can consist of a heavyweight trash bag or perhaps you would prefer to make use of one of those collapsible, spring-style containers in which you can place a liner bag of some kind. Whatever you choose, you need to plan to bring something for the purpose. No matter what kind of container you might use, either it or the liner bag will need to be disposed of whenever you and your crew leave camp.

Remember that it isn't just the nocturnal critters who may seek food at your campsite. By the way, a trash bag tied to a tree branch is no challenge at all for a squirrel and one on the ground might be viewed as a gift by an opossum. Either animal is capable of spreading the contents far and wide.

The trash bags you use at home might not be suitable for camping use. Depending upon where you camp you may need to carry a full bag to a somewhat distant dumpster or might need to keep the trash in your car. In either instance you would be likely to prefer to use bags that are a bit stronger and tougher than those you use in your kitchen at home. The bags designed for yard waste are often, but not always, somewhat stronger. Many are close to 1 Mil thick. "Contractor" trash bags, such as may be found at a home improvement store, usually range from 3 to 6 Mil in thickness and are the strongest you are likely to find.

Contractor trash bags are also large enough and tough enough to use for a variety of other purposes. For instance, if you were to want to sleep out under the stars you could place one of them under your sleeping bag for protection from possible condensation seepage from beneath. With a snip here and there, one could also be used as a durable, emergency rain poncho. A large trash bag could also be used as a waterproof cover for the firewood or kindling. In snow or on a steep, grassy slope a sturdy trash bag might be used as a sled upon which to carry firewood. I have even used a heavy-duty trash bag as my personal sled!

MEAL PLANNING and PREPARATION

One of the limiting factors for camp meal planning can be the lack of refrigeration. Or at least it could be after a couple of days unless plenty of ice is available. If you are rough camping in the far reaches of, say, a national forest, then you will likely need to make use of whatever is in your cooler (if you brought one) during the first day or two of your trip. It is, of course, possible to plan to use foods that require no refrigeration at all. Many improvements have been made to the varieties unrefrigerated foods, particularly to dried foods, over the years. Availability has also become much less of an issue. Many can now be found not only at outfitters but also at neighborhood grocery stores.

Dried Foods

There are some options when it comes to selecting dried foods. They consist of two main varieties, those that are simply air/heat dried, and foods that are freeze-dried. Dried foods are those that have been dehydrated through exposure to direct sunlight or slow, even heating at relatively low temperatures. Dried fruit, such as raisins and dates, are among the former group; packaged main courses, desserts, or even complete meals comprise the latter.

Your local grocery store probably carries a number of dried fruits that can be eaten as they are or can be re-hydrated according to the directions found on the package or by soaking them in water for a short time. You may not readily think of packaged noodles or instant rice as dried foods, but of course, that is what they are. Virtually every college student knows all about Ramen noodles, for instance. Some dried foods undergo changes of certain flavor and physical characteristics due to chemical changes that occur during the drying process. Because of this the flavor of some dried foods may be more intense, while the flavor of others can be lacking.

When they are rehydrated not all dried foods perform quite the same way as when they were fresh. Some, powdered eggs for instance, are said to work as well or even better than fresh in certain applications. Many freeze-dried vegetables, entrees and meals can be reasonably tasty when prepared according to directions.

There is a broad selection of meal possibilities among freeze-dried meal possibilities including omelets, Tex-Mex, and Oriental-style entrees. The packaging of some of these meals sometimes can be used in which to prepare them. There is even freeze-dried ice cream!

Other Non-Refrigerated Foods

Instant hot chocolate, instant coffee, powdered milk and Tang, for example, require nothing more than the addition of water to make them ready for consumption. The first two, of course, require very hot water. I have found that if powdered milk is made into liquid form for drinking it seems to taste better if made ahead and refrigerated for at least an hour. If the powdered milk is to be added to something else then the refrigeration would not be needed to develop the flavor.

The individually boxed juices with the little straws attached and some similarly packaged drinks need no refrigeration. You might need to convince kids that they taste even better that way! Although most people prefer them cold, canned or bottled soft drinks and bottled water need not be refrigerated.

Nuts of almost any kind can be a welcome snack or even a garnish to a dish. You may also consider seeds, such as pumpkin seeds. Roasted and then spiced, pumpkin seeds or *pepitas* are extremely popular as a snack food in Mexico. Look for *pepitas* in the international section of your grocery store or make your own. Recipes I have seen usually recommend drizzling a little oil on the raw pumpkin seeds then oven roasting at 350° on a cookie sheet for about 15 minutes or until golden and crunchy. Before the seeds cool, sprinkle them with some salt and chili pepper or with cinnamon sugar to taste.

Note that anyone in your crew who has a tree nut or peanut allergy should make all others in the group aware and should give instructions as to what steps to take if an allergen is somehow inadvertently consumed.

Potatoes, cabbage, onions, tomatoes, squashes, bell or other peppers, and a vast number of fruits do not require refrigeration but keep better if stored in a cool area.

Ready-to-eat bacon can be found at your local grocery as can salami, pepperoni, summer sausage, and jerky. All of these store best at normal room temperatures.

In the canned foods department of your local grocery store you can find numerous packages of dry soup mix that only require the addition of boiling water, but read the instructions carefully. Some require additional ingredients.

Parmesan cheese, either whole or pre-grated and stored in a baggie, keeps very well for weeks if it is not exposed to hot weather.

Many breakfast cereals can be eaten right out of the box. Other cereals of the instant variety, such as grits, oatmeal, and cream of wheat, may need to be stirred into some boiling water.

Plain crackers and most cookies keep well if kept from moisture. Watch out, though, for chocolate coated cookies or cookies containing chocolate chips. They are likely to become quite messy in hot weather.

If candy is going to make a trip in hot weather the possibility of melting ought to be considered. Most hard candies can survive almost any normal temperatures. Jelly beans can also be good for the purpose but your hands may show colorful evidence of eating them if the weather is hot.

The majority of individually tightly wrapped caramels or toffee-like candies will do well under most conditions so long as they are protected from getting squashed at the bottom of a backpack or food box.

Squishy, commercially sold breads won't transport well unless boxed in some way. Hard crusted, bakery breads may also need protection. Ask if the baker can slice the loaves for you in order to save effort when preparing a camp meal.

You will discover many creative uses for flour tortillas as well as for English muffins, if you bring them.

Many sauce or gravy mixes can add a little zest to certain dishes, but be sure to read the instructions to be sure of what must be added to the mixes.

Dried lentils, instant mashed potatoes, and quinoa cook up quite quickly in boiling water.

As you can see there are numerous options that are available to you. Just look through your grocery aisles with new eyes to find the dried foods there.

As a rule, store-bought eggs will spoil fairly quickly if unrefrigerated. However, unwashed eggs, directly from the farm, will usually keep for a few days without refrigeration because of a natural, antibiotic coating. The eggs should be washed before use, though.

Unrefrigerated Canned Foods

There is an astonishing assortment of canned foods or foods vacuum-sealed in jars from which to choose that require no refrigeration.

Canned meats include chipped beef, DAK precooked ham, corned beef, and Spam (which also comes in envelopes containing two slices.)

Canned fish (some of which also come in envelopes) such as tuna, smoked herring, and sardines are available.

It would be difficult to name a vegetable or fruit that can't be found in cans or jars. Take warning that the flavors of some canned vegetables are often very different that the flavors of the fresh ones. There are some vegetables, though, that are specially prepared prior to canning. These include refried beans, baked beans, applesauce, fried onions, pickled beets, and peanut butter.

I will not attempt to list here the vast array of canned main dishes, such as beef stew and corned beef hash, except as a reminder to look for them at your grocery store. If you have never before eaten one that you would like to take camping, my suggestion is to sample it at home. Some are better than others and I have found a few to be perfectly horrid.

Please be careful when transporting items packed in glass jars. A few moments taken to safeguard them against possible breakage can pay off in preventing messy cleanup and ruining meal plans.

Examples of Easy, Unrefrigerated Meals

Breakfast can consist of some pieces of dried fruit stirred in with some of the boiling water used to prepare instant oatmeal. Instant coffee or cocoa can accompany the meal. I have often enjoyed a powdered instant espresso, stirred together with a good cocoa mix, on those occasions when preparing camp coffee was not feasible.

Peanut butter spread onto Triscuit crackers along with an apple makes for a quick lunch. A bottle of water or a soft drink would be just fine with this.

Skillet-toasted flour tortillas covered with canned meat sauce, a light sprinkle of garlic powder and shredded Parmesan cheese could be a good camp-style pizza. Some canned pears might be a good, contrasting side dish. Possibly a "glass" of Merlot (for the adults, of course) would contribute to making this a fine meal at the end of the day.

Cooking Oil, Vinegar, Condiments, and Seasonings

Unless you are camping in a fully outfitted RV or know your way around a Dutch oven, your cooking methods will likely be limited to using the grill or the skillet. Either one performs much more efficiently with the use of cooking oil. Although olive oil is more flavorful than other oils it does not perform well when exposed to high heat. Because much of skillet cooking consists of frying, a more heat-tolerant oil, such as canola oil, might be your best choice. This is not to say that olive oil wouldn't be a great addition to some meals if you have room to bring it.

Vinegar, especially white vinegar can be quite versatile in its use at camp or when preparing to camp. Besides its many uses in cooking it is handy in many other ways. As mentioned elsewhere, a few splashes of vinegar can disrupt an ant trail. If your tent smells a bit musty you can set an open container of vinegar inside it for a few hours, removing it a while before you want to use the tent for sleeping. Doing this can somewhat improve the smell; but will not kill the mold that is probably the culprit. To eliminate or at least to further reduce the smell of a stubborn mold you would need to wipe down the entire tent with a solution of 1 part vinegar to 2 parts water. (See the section on GETTING READY TO CAMP for more precise instructions.) A dab of vinegar on a mosquito bite can bring some relief to the itching. It is also soothing when gently blotted onto sunburned areas. Some people say that if a lantern mantle is soaked overnight in vinegar and allowed to dry the mantle will last longer and burn brighter. I have yet to try this, however, and am unsure if it truly works.

When planning meals some thought should be given to what condiments and which seasonings should accompany the serving or should be a part of the preparation. There are some foods that require little more than a dash each of salt and pepper. Others might be much improved by the addition of a pinch of oregano. Do you like a little hot sauce on certain foods? There are people who cannot consider eating a hamburger without some ketchup, relish, and a dollop of mayonnaise.

Rather than to bring countless bulky containers of condiments or seasonings it is sometimes better to re-package them into smaller ones that you have carefully labeled. Pay close attention to those that must be refrigerated after opening. Your grocer or even a convenience store may carry much smaller bottles or jars of some items you would only find at a grocery in sizes larger than you may need. If you often frequent drive-thru's or have prepared foods delivered, the small packets of jelly, mustard, soy sauce, honey, barbecue sauce, or even salt and pepper that are left over could be very handy to have in your camping pantry. Consider collecting them during what some would call "the off-season."

For some camp dishes you'll find it helpful to make up some seasoning mixes of your own. For instance, if you were planning to make something with a Southwestern flair, you could fill a small, plastic baggie or reusable spice jar with this:

Allan's Southwest Seasoning

- 1 tablespoon chili powder
- 2 teaspoons smoked paprika
- 1 teaspoon ground cumin
- 1/2 teaspoon crushed red pepper
- 2 teaspoons dried oregano
- 2 teaspoons ground coriander
- 1/4 teaspoon powdered chipotle chili pepper

- 1 teaspoon roasted garlic powder
- 2 teaspoons salt
- ½ teaspoon black pepper

Coolers and Unrefrigerated Food Transport

When choosing a cooler for use when camping a few things should be considered. The cooler should be large enough to hold the necessary items as well as the ice packs or frozen bottles of water you will use. No matter which you use, your choice of the means for refrigeration will perform better and will last longer if covered by a heavy cloth or towel. By using the cloth, you can peel back just a corner of it to locate the needed item rather than to expose the entire contents of the cooler to the warmer air. More than one cooler might be needed for longer stays or for larger families.

In order to make best use of a cooler all foods and drinks should be thoroughly refrigerated or even frozen before they are placed in the cooler. Minimally, a cooler should be at room temperature at the time of loading rather than being dragged out of a hot garage or attic at the last minute. You can greatly prolong the cooler's ability to do its job if you pre-chill the cooler by placing a spare ice pack or a large, frozen bottle of water inside of it for at least an hour before you load the cooler with food and drink. Experts agree that items will stay colder longer if ice packs are placed on top of the contents because cool air travels downward.

If loose ice is being used the pre-chilled items should be loosely packed in the cooler and then topped with lots ice. Despite what is held by some as common wisdom, water that accumulates as the ice melts does not need to be drained from the cooler. The cold water makes even better contact with the bottles and cans than does the ice, itself. Some items or at least those with packaging that could become soggy should be placed atop goods that are impervious to water. The use of a separate cooler for drinks will allow the food cooler to not be opened as often, thereby probably increasing the life of the ice or other cooling elements in use.

Excess air space in your cooler is the enemy of its capacity for keeping things cool. Fill empty spaces with dry towels or other clean cloths. I have even used air bubble packing material to fill the space, sometimes in conjunction with keeping glass containers safe from breakage.

The plastic containers (usually blue) that are sold as freezer packs for coolers are handy and work well. However, you can freeze some plastic bottles of water and get similar results. Only plastic bottles rather than glass bottles should be used for this purpose to prevent possible breakage and to increase portability. The bottles must also have screw-tops to prevent leakage as they thaw. When filling them, the bottles should never be filled completely, leaving room for the water to expand as it freezes. My own preference is to freeze bottles of water with the lids removed, replacing the lids once the contents are completely frozen. Gallon or half-gallon jugs of water work extremely well for this purpose. The added advantage of using frozen bottles of water is that when thawed the drinking water inside is ready for consumption.

Where possible, one-time-use items designated for each meal, things that will not be returned to the cooler, should occupy one area of the cooler. Items used more often should be placed in the remaining space. This will make items easier to locate and so will help to minimize the time the cooler is open to the warmer air. It is advisable to very clearly label all containers, especially those holding components for a particular meal, so that needed items can more easily be located and can quickly be removed from the cooler. Layering items in order of planned use can be helpful, too, if it is possible. (See the section on Time Savers in CAMP COOKING.)

Sturdy, cardboard boxes can be used to transport unrefrigerated foods as well as such things as paper plates, cooking implements, pans, etc.. However, cardboard can become useless when in contact with moisture. Many experienced campers use large, plastic tubs or plastic boxes with tight-fitting lids for transporting dry goods. Plastic tubs or boxes can be very useful in that they can be placed upon the ground without the worry of moisture being absorbed. Many such containers have built-in hand holds that make it easy to return the containers to the car or truck after a meal. (See also the section on What to Carry It In, in the section on EQUIPMENT.)

CAMP COOKING

Methods, hints of ingredients, and the recipes given here are my own or were combined from recipes found in a number of sources. My apologies to vegans reading this because much of what will be found in this section consists of meat-based foods I have prepared and eaten when camping and reflect my own preferences. Most of the camp cooking I have done has been through the use of a campfire or on a camp stove and will likely be reflected in what you will be reading. It is worth noting as you read this section to bear in mind that camping seems to lend itself to big appetites. Plan accordingly.

For many campers, some of their best memories have much to do with the meals or treats they ate while camping. Cooking at camp can be similar to, but usually quite different from the cooking done at home. For instance, not everyone is accustomed to cooking on a gas burner, over an open fire, or without a refrigerator nearby. Not only can the methods be different but also the foods, themselves, may also be other than the normal fare. Because of these and other factors, camp cooking requires a divergent mindset as well as some skills that will develop over time but may seem quite novel at first.

Camp cooking takes time to learn. While cooking at camp can be challenging or even difficult, a great amount of pride and satisfaction can be gleaned from the making of a good camp meal. Some processes are easier to master than others because of similarities to those done at home. However, at camp the making something as deceptively simple as toast can be a challenge and the order in which foods must be prepared may be unusual. Mistakes are sure to be made - even by the more experienced camp cooks. The real trick is in working around the challenges one must overcome to avoid producing foods that are inedible and wasting the precious, limited supply of food.

When wilderness tent camping in areas where there is danger of large predators, such as grizzlies, invading your camp, you should plan to do your cooking and eating a few hundred feet away from where your sleeping quarters are located. In this way you can at least partially prevent the scent of food attracting unwanted attention in the middle of the night. (Please see the section on Raccoons, Squirrels, Chipmunks, Skunks, Etc. in the section on WILDLIFE.)

Whether you do your cooking in your RV or plan to use a camp stove or the campfire for cooking meals, the simpler the meal is, the more time you have to enjoy other activities. On the other hand, if you are up to the challenge of cooking a gourmet meal and consider that as part of your camping experience, that's just fine, too. Your choice of cooking equipment and recipes depends greatly upon what style of cooking you wish to use. Also, you might find that camp menus may not be quite as well balanced as they probably are at home. In the long run, a few days' disruption of the norm will do no permanent harm and is part of the fun. My own preference is to leave the gourmet stuff for when I am at home and for the most part, to keep camp cooking simple. This is not to say a certain amount of creativity can't be employed when making meals. I have prepared a lobster dinner at camp, but I have also eaten baked beans right out of the can. Your main limiting factor is your imagination.

I have a special place in my heart for cast iron cookware and have an ever-growing collection. Many years ago, I only had two pieces. They were very large (No. 10) skillets, the cooking surface measuring a bit more than 12 inches in diameter. I brought both of them with me on a camping trip in which to bake a pizza. First, I thoroughly heated both skillets over the campfire. After removing the skillets from the fire, I slid a store-bought, prepared, 12-inch pizza into one of the hot skillets and then covered it with the second inverted skillet and set the makeshift oven aside on a large, flat rock. Approximately twenty minutes later my crude pizza oven proved to have worked exactly as intended. Some years later I acquired a huge Dutch oven that is much better suited for such a task. True, the aforementioned meal was not at all gourmet in substance, but I believe the method demonstrated a fair degree of creativity.

Camp Coffee

Some of us require coffee to start our day. In my opinion there is no better form in which to enjoy that wonderful potion than that of camp coffee. The making of camp coffee is perhaps the most basic of all of the many methods of creating what I think of as a staple of any morning and certainly of a morning at camp.

- To a pot add almost enough drinkable water equal to the amount of coffee you wish to make.
- Leave a small amount of cool water aside for later use.
- Bring the water in the pot to a boil.
- Remove the pot from the fire.
- Add regular or drip grind coffee to the pot in proportion to the amount of water.
- Stir the grounds into the heated water.
- Allow the coffee to brew for a minimum of four minutes.
- Generously sprinkle the surface of the brewed coffee with the cool water. The addition of the cool water will cause the coffee grounds to sink to the bottom of the pot.
- Serve.

Keep in mind that the resulting drink is likely to be a little thicker than customary. Also, you may find a smidgen of grounds at the bottom of your cup when you take that last sip. I think it is a great excuse to rinse your cup and pour another cupful.

Time Savers

One of the most time-consuming parts of camping can be meal preparation. Sometimes it can seem that you have just finished cleaning up after one meal when it is time to begin to prepare another. The time spent in food preparation can be daunting, particularly if everything must be made "from scratch." One thing is as true at camp as it is at home: Reheating foods is faster and easier than the initial cooking of them. Well in advance of your camping trip, whenever you make a one-pot meal at home, consider the notion of doubling the recipe and freezing half. What could be easier at camp than to pull a storage container out of the cooler and to reheat its contents in a single pot or skillet over the fire?

Actually, there is an answer to that question. What if the container were to hold something that requires no heating? Explore possible use of dishes that are normally served cold like macaroni or Greek pasta salad. By adding a few things to dishes such as these, virtually complete, one-dish meals can be made ahead. A hummus dip served with fresh vegetables can make for a great lunch. There are also some tasty, cold soups that could be welcome on a hot day. Of course, sandwiches and wraps alone can be nearly complete meals. You might even be able to just set out the "makin's" for your crew and let them help themselves!

You can also save time, mess, and effort at camp through the use of pre-mixed ingredients. Bisquick or Jiffy All-Purpose Baking Mix are extremely versatile products with which you can not only make biscuits but also pancakes through the addition of nothing more than water or milk and eggs. Other easy mixes are also available.

Alternatively, you can make some of your own mixes in advance of your camping trip. For items such as biscuits or pancakes you can put together all of the dry ingredients, possibly including powdered eggs and/or powdered milk, in a sturdy, plastic-zippered storage bag to which you need only add water and perhaps a splash of oil. (Be sure to calculate the extra water needed for the rehydration of the powdered milk and powdered eggs.) Once you have added the wet ingredients to whatever dry mix you use, squeeze the bag enough to mix everything and you are set to skillet-bake your creation. Also, be sure to clearly label all pre-mixes you might make as to what they are, what must be added to them, for which day, and for which meal they are to be used. For instance:

PANCAKE MIX
TUESDAY - BREAKFAST
ADD ONE EGG, 1 C. MILK, 2 TBSP OIL

Much troublesome effort can be avoided by doing some prep work beforehand. If one or more of the meals you anticipate making at camp involves chopped vegetables, try chopping and bagging them the day before you leave on your trip. If you have plans, for instance, to make a stew you can cut up the carrots, celery, and onions and put them all together in a baggie. You can even cut up potatoes in advance, but only if you coat them with a little cooking oil to preserve them and then possibly bag them separately. The meat can be cut to size, floured, and bagged. Then all of the components can be placed in a larger bag labeled, "STEW" and possibly even marked as "THURSDAY - SUPPER" if that is your plan. Even a packet of seasonings you might wish to use can be included in the larger package. Think about the meals you plan so you can see if there are other ways you can simplify the assembly of your camp meals.

There are also some substitutions or modifications you can use to make meals easier or at least different. Being creative may require some extra cleverness on your part, but that's part of the fun. For instance, individual camp pizzas can be made using thin slices of toasted English muffins as pizza crusts. Perhaps you could use mashed avocado where you might normally use mayonnaise. Or, you could replace the slices of bread of a sandwich by using tortillas to create wraps or burritos. In the cold foods (such as cheese and eggs) area of your grocery store you might have noticed packages of shredded potatoes with which to make hash browns. With just a little imagination you'll find many other ways in which those potatoes might be used.

The Easiest Meals

At camp any meal that can be prepared with a minimum of effort is a good one. It always seems as though there is not enough time to cook the meals because of the other fun there is to be had. The most obvious way around that problem is to plan meals that require as little preparation as possible. As was mentioned elsewhere, having meals that only require heating can help to save time and effort. But meals that don't even require heating are even better! Better still are the meals that the other campers in your crew make for themselves.

At the risk of repeating what was already said in the section on Time Savers, foods that you have already prepared and frozen at home are great for use at camp. Maybe you made some Louisiana-style red beans and rice or some minestrone soup that you froze. What welcome meal makers either of those could be at the end of a busy day at camp! Just heat and serve!

One Pot Meals

Making single pot meals can simplify camp cooking, particularly if some of the ingredients are prepared ahead of time. For instance, you can brown a pound of hamburger, pork sausage, or ground turkey at home ahead of time for use in making a variety of simple dishes. I like to stir in some finely chopped onion along with the meat as it browns. Of course, you can certainly brown the meat at camp if you prefer, but we're talking about keeping it simple.

One thing you could make is Campfire Spaghetti. Into a large pot add two 24 oz. jars of spaghetti sauce. Add about two or three cups of the browned meat. Refill both jars with clean water and add the water to the pot. (Be somewhat sparing with the water.) Add some Italian seasonings if you wish. You can even stir in some chopped slices of pepperoni, if desired - skimping on the salt and pepper if you do. Bring the mixture to a low boil. Add 1 lb. of spaghetti noodles (broken in half to fit the pot if necessary) along with salt and pepper to taste. Being sure to stir occasionally, allow the pot to simmer for about 15 minutes or until the noodles are cooked to the desired consistency. Serve with grated Parmesan cheese.

A one pot meal called Camp-style Baked Beans can be as simple as dumping a can or two of baked beans into a pot and adding hot dogs or even smoked sausages that have been cut into bite-size pieces. Bring the mixture to a simmer for a few minutes and your main dish is ready to eat.

Another one to try is Camping Chili. To a large pot add two 16 oz. cans of prepared chili and a 10 oz. Can of ROTEL Diced Tomatoes & Green Chilies. Stir the mixture to blend then bring to a simmer. Top with a layer of ½ inch slices of polenta followed by a topping of grated cheddar cheese. Cover and allow to cook at a low heat until the polenta slices are soft and the cheese is melted. You can also skip the polenta and just pour the chili over some tortilla chips.

No Cook Meals

Breakfast can be as simple as some yogurt sprinkled with chopped nuts and served with some whole fresh fruit. Also, I've been told you can mix equal parts of rolled oats and milk into a lidded container that you place in the cooler overnight. In the morning add some fruit and/or cinnamon and breakfast is ready! You can find online many useful recipes for making breakfast "muffins" many of which are full of numerous breakfast staples including hash brown potatoes, eggs, and sausage or bacon. Some are quite suitable for making ahead for your camp breakfasts.

Lunch or even dinner meals can be variations on the idea of a platter of crackers, cheese, vegetables, and a dip or peanut butter. How about a plate loaded with alternating slices of boiled egg, (which you had the foresight to boil ahead at home) sliced tomatoes, and slices of mozzarella cheese? You could sprinkle a little salt and pepper along with some dried basil or oregano over it. Cold cuts can also be set out along with sliced cheese, bread, and condiments for a quick serve-yourself meal. Of course, almost any foods that don't require cooking can easily become major components of a make-your-own meal. All you need to do is to lay out the ingredients and to let folks have at it!

Cooking Over A Fire

My own preference is to cook over a campfire whenever possible, but campfire cooking often requires a more leisurely schedule than is sometimes allowed by other activities. It also requires careful planning and attention. Preparing a campfire for cooking can also call for patience. A campfire has three main stages once it has been successfully ignited. At first it burns with very high and bright flames. After a while it burns down to flames that lick the wood from the beginnings of a bed of coals beneath. Later on, the wood gradually transforms to a bed of glowing coals with flames appearing only now and again.

When the fire is brightly flaming is usually the best time to put a pot on to boil. You can use a flaming hot fire for making coffee, for boiling corn-on-the-cob, or maybe for boiling water for later dish washing. Once the flames die down a bit you can use them for the frying of eggs or sausage or for browning chunks of beef or cubes of tofu. When the fire is reduced to a thick bed

of glowing coals, it is ready for broiling and roasting or for slower cooking. Now is the best time to put on the burgers, steaks, or fish. However, no broiling or roasting should be attempted until the cooking grate is brushed clean and is wiped with a paper towel or brush soaked in cooking oil. This is particularly true when grilling fish. Fish seem to become one with a grill. For that reason, it might be a good idea to spread a little oil directly onto the fish as well as onto the grill.

Learning to judge your fire and how to take the best advantage of its stages takes a little practice. Some people prefer to do almost all of their cooking over hot coals. This can best be done by making use of what is called a "keyhole" fire or else by creating two fire zones within your fire ring. (See the section on "The Shape of Your Fire" in the CAMPFIRE section.)

A keyhole fire consists of a round fire area that has a smaller, somewhat rectangular section added to the circumference, giving the open fire its namesake shape. The main fire takes up the larger section. As the main fire burns down, its coals can be pushed into the smaller one. The latter is used for the majority of the cooking. More coals can be pushed into the smaller section as needed.

The iron fire rings at most campgrounds aren't conducive to this configuration but an improvisation can be accomplished. Start your fire in the large part of the fire ring not covered by the grate. As your fire produces coals you can relocate a few of them at a time so they are under the fire grate. Now you are ready to roast or broil or simmer. Add more coals from the main fire as required.

Depending upon your menu, you might start a small fire in the area under the grate or in the smaller portion of your keyhole in order to boil or rapidly heat something using the grate and then make use of the diminishing heat to do the rest of your cooking.

Aluminum Foil Cooking

Aluminum foil is useful in camp cooking to make self-contained meals or side dishes, as well as some delicious desserts, while saving the cleanup crew from the mess the use of pots and pans might create.

Aluminum foil comes in two thicknesses, regular and heavy-duty. The heavy-duty foil is the more useful for camp cooking, but regular-thickness foil can be used by the addition of a second layer. Enclosing the food in an envelope or package is the method most employed. After the item to be cooked is placed near the center of half of a large sheet of foil. Fold the empty half over the food and seal the edges by crimping. I usually double-crimp by folding over about a half inch of the long edge and then fold that over once again, doing much the same operation on each of the other edges.

- An ear of corn, once shucked and smeared with butter, can be wrapped in foil and placed on the coals for about 8 minutes. Be sure to turn the corn at least once as it cooks.

- A seasoned chicken quarter can be sealed together with a few slices of sweet potato and/or orange to make for part of a tasty meal. Cooking time on the coals is between half and three quarters of an hour. The package should be turned often.

- Peel a peach and cut it in half using its crease as a guide. Remove the seed. Push some softened butter into the two recesses left by the seed. Sprinkle both halves with a mixture of cinnamon and sugar. Reassemble the two halves. Wrap in foil and seal. Cook for about a quarter of an hour, turning occasionally.

When cooking more than one item in the same envelope cooking time should be estimated according to the item needing to cook the longest. Don't crowd the items in the envelopes. Leave enough space for them to expand or to release steam as they cook.

Some samples of approximate cooking times:

Broccoli spears 7-10 minutes
Whole fish 15-20 minutes
Pork chops 20-30 minutes

Whole potatoes 45-60 minutes (Don't forget to pierce them before sealing them in the foil.)

Cooking time will vary, depending greatly upon the heat of the fire. Because peeking is inadvisable, many food items may turn out even better if left for a little longer instead of a shorter time. Some items, especially fish, might be prone to sticking to the foil. Sticking can be prevented by smearing the inside portion of the foil with butter or oil. At least one brand of aluminum foil offers non-stick products. They are said to work fine on a grill, but are somewhat expensive compared to regular foil.

Often you will find that something can be eaten directly out of the foil package by simply using a knife to slice an X on the upward side and carefully peeling the envelope open from the center of the X. Be careful! Hot steam is likely to escape from the opening.

I have seen a few clever campers who made some foil-pack dinners just prior to leaving home to go camping. In this way they had meals that could cook over the campfire's coals while camp was being set up and would be ready to eat as soon as the work was done.

There is something that should be kept in mind when cooking with aluminum foil, particularly if foil packages are made ahead of time. Acidic foods such as tomato sauce or chopped onions as well as strongly seasoned or highly salty foods can create conditions that might cause pitting in aluminum foil over time. This is not to say that such things cannot be used in aluminum foil if cooked soon afterward, only that the reactive foods do not store well in the foil.

Cooking on A Stick

There's something quite special about roasting food on a stick. It is perhaps the most basic, primal means of cooking there is. You can use store-bought roasting sticks for the purpose, but I think doing so is somehow less elemental feeling.

If you should forget to bring your store-bought sticks or just want to use a more fundamental method, there are some things to keep in mind. If at all possible, you should select thin sections of branches that are of dry and aged wood. It is best that you have some idea as to what sort of tree the branches are from. It is possible to find branches that it would be unwise to use. Green wood should be avoided because, especially when it is heated, disagreeable flavors may be transmitted to the food being cooked.

Whether to use a straight or a forked stick is usually a matter of personal preference, but could also depend upon what food is to be roasted. The branch should be substantial enough to support the weight of the food to be cooked. To further preclude possible unpleasant flavor transfers as well as to expose a cleaner part of the wood, all traces of bark must be removed from the portion of the stick that will contact the food. Dependent upon what is to be roasted, the tip of the roasting end could also be sharpened. Once the stick is otherwise ready, the bare end should be briefly put into the flames of the fire to sear the wood and to further ensure its cleanliness. Now you are ready to use your roasting stick!

Nearly everyone is aware that marshmallows are traditionally roasted on a stick over a campfire's glowing bed of coals. Stick-roasted hot dogs are also camping treats. But there are some other things that are fun to prepare by fire roasting. For instance, a bit of biscuit dough, whether from a store-bought roll from the grocery or from dough made at camp, can be rolled into a thick "snake" and then coiled in a loose spiral around the end of your stick, impaling the end of the dough upon the point of the stick. Then the dough can be roasted until golden. This is a delicious, fun way to make biscuits and can involve every member of the family. (See also the recipe for Bannock below.)

While it is certainly true that you can toast marshmallows at a blazing fire, it is easier for small kids to get near the glowing coals of a fire than an intensely hot fire in the earlier stages. Roasting over the coals also makes it easier to actually toast the marshmallows rather than to set them on fire - unless that is your preference. (Please also see the section on Marshmallows in the section on CAMPFIRE/Fire Safety.)

I should mention that despite recommendations I have seen, roasting a steak or chicken quarter on a forked stick might not be as wonderful an idea as you might be led to believe. Just getting the steak evenly skewered on the stick can be a challenge. Chicken takes a long time to cook, usually much longer than you would want to stand and hold that stick over the fire. In both examples there is an ever-present danger of the stick's breaking or of the meat sliding off the stick and into the fire. In addition, one part of the meat can easily end up being well-cooked long before another.

Camp Desserts

For most kids (of any age,) the making of s'mores is nearly synonymous with the notion of camping. The younger children revel in the idea of creating something delicious "all by themselves."

For the uninitiated, your main job is to lay out the ingredients and possibly to help with final assembly. All that is needed is some roasting sticks, (Please see the above section, Cooking on A Stick.) a bag of marshmallows, a plate filled with graham cracker squares and another plate filled with flat pieces of solid chocolate candy bars of a size that will fit onto the cracker squares. Once a marshmallow has been roasted it is removed from the roasting stick onto one of the cracker squares upon which a chocolate piece is then placed. At that point a second graham cracker square is put on top to make a sweet, gooey, and deliciously messy sandwich. A wise camper will have a damp washcloth or paper towel at hand to wipe sticky fingers and mouths. (Also see the section on MARSHMALLOWS under CAMPFIRE/Fire Safety.)

Most kids simply will never tire of having s'mores at camp. However, you can create a bit of variety by offering some other treats such as Chocolate Banana Boats. Without peeling the banana, cut a slit along its length with the knife penetrating only halfway through. Push chocolate morsels through the peel and into the slit of the banana. If you wish, you can alternate the chocolate morsels with miniature marshmallows. Then, making sure to have the split side upward, place the stuffed banana into the coals of the campfire. Allow approximately 10-15 minutes cooking time for the chocolate to melt. Using tongs, carefully remove the cooked banana from the fire. Dust off all ashes or wipe them off with a damp paper towel. Then push the ends of the banana toward the middle to open it as you would with a baked potato. Allow to cool slightly, then serve with a spoon.

See the section on Aluminum Foil Cooking to find the recipe for baking a peach. Instead of using the cinnamon and sugar, try stuffing the seed cavity with a miniature marshmallow or two along with an unwrapped piece of caramel candy.

Skillet Baking

Although many people recognize that making pancakes is a form of baking that makes use of a skillet, not everyone knows of other methods of skillet-baking.

Once while canoe camping, I baked in an aluminum mess kit I had. I used an instant mix to make a batch of biscuit dough and placed the entire lump into the skillet half of the mess kit. My mess kit had a matching skillet-like piece that could be clamped over the other half. Having attached the tightly fitting piece that now served as a lid, I placed the assembly in the coals of the campfire. To keep the dough from getting scorched I turned the mess kit over every few minutes until I judged that the dough was fully cooked - probably about fifteen minutes. My canoeing companion and I carefully unclamped and removed the lid to reveal a golden brown, giant biscuit! We broke open the middle of the biscuit and found somewhat to our surprise that the dough was baked completely. Then we dumped some jelly into the opening and began to feast. What a treat!

You might try a similar feat using a somewhat different method. A staple among many Native Americans in times gone by is what has become known as bannock. Indians probably used something other than wheat flour long ago and could also have added a few other ingredients that might have included dried fruits or dried meat, for instance. The recipe here is more modern; but the traditional method for baking this bread is not greatly different from what is described here. Note that an iron skillet would probably work best for this recipe. Other skillets can be used, but beware that plastic handles might melt during lengthy exposure to heat.

Bannock

- 2 cups multi-purpose flour
- 1 tablespoon baking powder
- ½ teaspoon salt
- 2 tablespoons sugar

These ingredients can be mixed ahead. Then when ready to make the bannock add:

- ¼ cup oil or shortening

(For a richer consistency a single beaten egg can also be added before adding other liquids.)

- 2 cups water or milk - add a little at a time to avoid making the dough too sticky

Place the dough into an ungreased skillet and spread it to cover the skillet evenly. Prop the skillet so it is not quite vertical but is very close to a fire that has burned down to a thick bed of coals. Turn the propped skillet clockwise or counter-clockwise periodically to ensure even baking to a golden brown.

Total baking time can be about 15-20 minutes but could vary greatly depending upon the heat of the fire. Note that if the skillet doesn't feel hot to the touch after a few minutes its distance from the fire or else the fire itself might need adjusting.

Although this baking method can be used, the bannock can also be fry-baked in a lightly greased skillet, carefully turning once as the underside becomes browned. (Also, please see Cooking on A Stick under CAMP COOKING.)

Leftovers

As was said above, appetites tend to be big among campers. However, you might occasionally find yourself having to deal with leftovers. If you considered this possibility when you planned your meals you will have on hand containers for the uneaten food. You may surprise yourself at how creatively you might use some of the leftovers to augment or to accompany a future meal. For breakfast, leftover chili might be the perfect thing to plate along with fried eggs and leftover mashed potatoes. Get creative!

BREAKING CAMP

"Pulling up stakes" as the expression goes, is not usually the first step to breaking camp. There is a logical order in which to do all that needs to be done. The most important thing to know is when to begin breaking camp. This is particularly true if your camping spot is in an organized campground where there is a set check-out time.

Consider for a moment the condition of the campsite when you first arrived. In many campgrounds you might have found the site free of litter, the tent pad clear of debris and possibly even raked, the fire ring free of partially burned remnants of the previous occupant's fire, and the table clear of food scraps or other litter. In such well-tended campgrounds, the check-out time is set to allow personnel time to restore campsites to a presentable condition before future campers check in. What this means to you is that you must plan to have your campfire "dead out" and all of your equipment and crew packed up and rolling out of the campground no later than the appointed check-out time.

Most campers like to enjoy one last meal before they break camp. Usually, this is lunch because in many campgrounds the check-out time is in the early afternoon. Unless a fire's warmth is needed, it is best to have that last meal planned such that no campfire cooking would be involved. This allows some time for the morning's campfire (if one were set at all) to burn down to a point at which it will be simpler to extinguish.

Extinguishing the campfire is often left as a last step or is too often forgotten altogether. Actually, it should be first on the list. By tending to this early there is plenty of time to monitor it to ensure that the fire is completely out. The process usually involves at least a gallon of water. Pour, stir, check; pour, stir, check. (Please see Put Your Fire Out in CAMPFIRE.)

If you are tent camping, the next step is to remove anything inside your tent and pack it all into your vehicle. You are likely to discover that these items won't fit into your vehicle quite the same way as they did when you packed at home, because you now have a bag filled with whatever clothing you have made use of during your stay. Be sure you also have a plastic bag available to accommodate wet swimwear, beach towels, etc., that might have been used for that final farewell swim.

Once the tent is clear of its former contents it is a good idea to have a whisk broom on hand with which to sweep out any sand, leaves, or dirt that could have found a way in. Some smaller tents, once the stakes have been pulled, can simply be lifted up and shaken out.

Some camping books and equipment manufacturers will advise leaving windows and doors unzipped before striking (taking down) the tent. On the surface this seems logical, as the openings allow trapped air to escape more readily as the tent is folded. However, imagine for a moment that it is starting to rain as your next camping adventure begins. Do you really want the interior of the tent wetted as you race to set it up? For this reason, when you take down the tent, I suggest zipping all zippers and securing all flaps as though it were raining. If you push down as you fold or roll up your tent, you'll find that the air escapes without much difficulty.

Oh, but what if it is actually raining when you break camp? It is a good idea to plan to have enough large, plastic or waterproof bags on hand in which to transport clothing, sleeping bags, and such to the vehicle. (Remember those big bags we discussed in the section on TRASH? Here is another reason for having them.) It is also good to have such a bag in which to put a sopping wet tent - bearing in mind that you must remember to completely dry the tent as soon as is at all possible to prevent mold or mildew.

Tent drying can be accomplished even in a small apartment by spreading the tent as much as possible and by periodically turning it over and over again until all parts of it are absolutely dry. Be sure to place a plastic tarp under the tent as you dry it indoors to preclude the possibility of its staining your carpet or furniture.

Speaking of dampness, as soon as you have your tent folded you will almost invariably find that the underside of your tent's footprint or ground cloth is wet. If weather permits you should allow this to dry before packing it away. If necessary, though, you can dry it later when, and in much the same way as, you dry your tent.

If a final meal is to be had at camp and you haven't already had it, now is the time. The hardest part of breaking camp is done and little remains except to pack away the rest of the food, plates, napkins and such. When all is put away and you are almost ready to drive away, take a very careful look around the campsite to see if any small items or litter are present. You may discover an errant tent stake or a plastic spoon someone accidentally dropped. Did you remember to put the table back where it was when you arrived? How about that tablecloth? Ready? Roll your vehicle forward a bit and check where it once was. Grab that last bag of trash and take it to the appropriate bin or stash it in your vehicle.

Take one last look at your campsite. Would you want to arrive and find the campsite looking as it does? My own belief, especially when camping in a remote area, is to leave the area in such a manner that few would ever recognize that anyone had ever camped there before.

Now you're ready for the ride home. If you are at a campground, please be sure to deposit your check-out envelope or hang-tag or otherwise let it be known you are leaving. The next camper might be anxiously awaiting the start of a new camping adventure.

CAMP HOSTS - WHAT ARE THEY? WHAT DO THEY DO?

The number of campers who have no idea what camp hosts are or what they do or even that they exist shouldn't surprise me. I was one such camper only a few years ago.

I have not yet found a resource that nails down when it was that the concept of camp hosts began. My best guess is that it originated not long after recreational camping gained popularity. It is my belief that organized campgrounds were originally little more than "mom and pop" enterprises. As camping became more and more popular the campground owners probably needed additional help in keeping up with such things as campground maintenance and tending to the camp store. Some campground owners might not have been able to afford to pay a salary in exchange for help. Instead they may have worked out a sort of barter, offering free lodging as payment for the assistance the "camp hosts" offered.

The system for payment of camp hosts has changed little since the beginnings. A free camping spot as well as free hookups to water, electricity, and sewer are often offered. In some campgrounds a salary is also included. A few campgrounds even offer extra enticements such as free tickets to local events or attractions.

The number of hours of work required of the camp hosts can vary greatly. Some campgrounds call for 40 hours per week while others require only 20 hours or even fewer. Not every campground makes use of camp hosts. Some, particularly the private campgrounds, prefer to make more permanent arrangements. This is likely because many camp hosts are somewhat transient, often working at a campground for just a short time and then moving on to another. Among campers who make use of RVs is a set for whom their RV is their home. These RVers are known as "full-timers," many of whom travel to warmer parts of the country when winter comes. Full-timers might host at a campground in Pennsylvania during the summer and then move to host at one in Florida when snow threatens.

Camp host work can also vary. Required work might include: picking up litter, emptying fire pits, raking leaves, painting, cleaning and stocking bathrooms, running the camp store, and office work such as registering campers. Often the work can include any or all of those tasks and more. Camp hosts are also usually expected to supply campers with information regarding campground rules, to give directions to and information about nearby trails, to inform campers about and often to assist with special activities, to report disruptive or unlawful activities to local authorities, and to assist campers in contacting emergency personnel when needed.

In recent years Carmen and I have volunteered as camp hosts at parks administered by state as well as by federal government. These experiences have allowed me countless opportunities to greatly appreciate the camping knowledge I have had the privilege of learning since my early childhood.

Because most things related to camping are by now almost second nature to both Carmen and me, it sometimes surprises us that there are so very many people for whom camping is a completely new adventure. We almost envy the inexperienced campers we encounter because they are so excited to learn this craft. Whenever possible and most especially when asked, we try to pass onto the campers we meet whatever bits of camping knowledge we have that might serve to make their camping adventures more pleasurable.

Most camp hosts have the desire to be as helpful as possible to campers while at the same time wanting to allow campers the peace and privacy to pursue their camping adventures undisturbed. Camp hosts love to answer questions or to give assistance. Make it a point to discover whether your campground has a camp host. Often you may find them sitting outside of their RV. Normally, there will be a placard posted that indicates their status as camp hosts. Strike up a conversation with them. They might be able to tell you something about the campground or about the area that you didn't know. Make use of them – whether for an emergency or simply for learning where to get firewood. They will be glad to be of help.

WE AREN'T DONE YET!

I am sure by now you know of my belief that every camping trip is different. Each is its own learning experience. The information I have assembled here is so much less than you will gather from your camping adventures. There is no end to learning about camping, just as you will never find any book anywhere that will tell you everything you need to know about it.

My hope is that you have found useful tips here and that you will have many, many opportunities to recall some of them as you have camping experiences of your own!